ISRAELI CULTURE BETWEEN
THE TWO INTIFADAS

Israeli Culture between the Two Intifadas

A BRIEF ROMANCE

Yaron Peleg

UNIVERSITY OF TEXAS PRESS
Austin

Requests for permission to reproduce material from this work
should be sent to:
Permissions
University of Texas Press
P.O. Box 7819
Austin, TX 78713-7819
www.utexas.edu/utpress/about/bpermission.html

♾ The paper used in this book meets the minimum requirements
of ANSI/NISO z39.48-1992 (R1997) (Permanence of Paper).

Library of Congress Cataloging-in-Publication Data

Peleg, Yaron.
    Israeli culture between the two Intifadas : a brief romance /
Yaron Peleg.—1st ed.
        p. cm.
    Includes bibliographical references and index.
    ISBN 978-0-292-71877-7 (cloth : alk. paper)
1. Love in literature.   2. Israeli fiction—History
and criticism.   3. Keret, Etgar, 1967—Criticism and
interpretation.   4. Taub, Gadi—Criticism and interpretation.
5. Weil, Uzi—Criticism and interpretation.   6. Amir, Gafna,
1966—Criticism and interpretation.   7. Israel—Intellectual
life—20th century.—I. Title.
    PN56.L6P39   2008
    892.4'36—dc22

                                        2008022372

This book is dedicated ברוך ואהבה, *with tenderness
and love, to my grandmother, Marta Peleg, who in her
own small way as a pioneering kibbutznik took part in
laying the foundations for Israeli culture and lived it
passionately throughout her long life.*

CONTENTS

PREFACE

Although I sat down to write this book about a year ago, the idea for it had been with me in one sense or another for more than ten years now. It was nurtured by the longing I felt for the Israel I left behind; it stood before me in the books I chose to read, and informed many of the courses I taught about Israeli literature and culture at Brandeis, Princeton, and George Washington University. Had I lived in Israel at that time I may not have noticed so readily the sweeping changes that transformed the country so much. But I lived far away, and the great distance from home and the sense of removal I felt from it sharpened my vision and at the same time drove me to bridge the gap by staying almost obsessively connected: I read several Israeli newspapers a day, watched newscasts, followed popular television programs, and remained connected to Israel in the many ways made possible by the rapidly growing Internet.

The great hopes of the Oslo years in the mid-1990s made my sense of removal deeper and more frustrating still. I was too young to be permanently impressed by the victory in the Six-Day War—I was seven at the time—and too old to believe that the 1982 war in Lebanon would really protect the Galilee—I was twenty-two at the time and on reserve duty for the first time. For my generation, then, Oslo seemed like the End of Days, that blissful time of peace with our Arab neighbors we were promised time and again since childhood. Being away from an Israel that seemed so cool and so "happening" was exasperating. This book was conceived as an attempt to channel these frustrations. The fact that the Oslo hopes did not materialize only makes their promise more alluring. I hope this book captures this promise and allure.

Boston
Summer 2007

ACKNOWLEDGMENTS

My deepest thanks go to my friend and colleague Eran Kaplan, of the University of Cincinnati, without whose extensive knowledge, sagacity, insight, and encouragement this book would not have taken the shape it has. As expatriate members of the "Oslo Generation" we tried to bring our far homeland closer by endlessly discussing it. Many of our discussions found their way into this book in one form or another and, one hopes, improved it. I also want to thank another colleague and friend, Gidi Nevo of Ben-Gurion University, for carefully reading the manuscript and giving me the benefit of his keen intellect. My partner, Mike, has been by far the greatest source of inspiration and encouragement. His passionate interest in Israel, his affinity for its people, and his remarkable feeling for its culture constantly challenge my own understanding and views, sharpening and focusing them in ways that I believe and hope have benefited this book very much.

ISRAELI CULTURE BETWEEN
THE TWO INTIFADAS

INTRODUCTION

The last two decades of the twentieth century brought profound changes to Israel and opened it up to increasing outside influences. Throughout the 1980s, the country also experienced accelerated economic development and the establishment of a Western, capitalist society, a trend which was expedited by the influx of hundreds of thousands of Russian immigrants in the early 1990s and symbolized by the signing of the Oslo Accord in 1993. These developments, the addition of nearly one million workers and consumers to Israel's economy, and the first real chance at peace with the entire Arab world, brought Israel much closer to Western consumerist society, exposed it to its popular culture, and began to change it in significant ways. The most notable of these changes was the apparent demise of Zionism, the powerful ideology which, in the span of merely fifty years, gave birth to Jewish nationalism and then to the modern state of Israel.[1]

The weakening hold of Zionist ideology was not necessarily a negative development. Many saw it as a sign of health that marked the country's maturity and signaled the next stage in its evolution. Like any liminal stage, however, it was a period that engendered fear, confusion, and doubt, all of which found concerned expression in the culture's literature. Since its strong ideological beginnings in the nineteenth century, modern Hebrew literature has often been used by readers to take the nation's pulse, as it were, to follow its development and understand its inner workings. This book attempts to do something similar, to examine what contemporary Israeli authors have to say about the alleged decline of a national ethos that united Jews for one hundred years and about the arrival of a post-national age in Israel.

One of the illustrative ways Hebrew literary critics characterized and distinguished literary generations from one another during
the past century has been to focus on the common use and function of
the narrative voice as an expression of the age.[2] Thus, the anguished
and introverted voice of the lonely first-person-singular narrator in many
works of the Hebrew Revival came to symbolize the hesitant and precarious beginnings of a new Hebrew culture in the Land of Israel at the
beginning of the twentieth century. Similarly, the first person plural of
the following literary generation, the *Yishuv* or 1948 Generation, came to
symbolize the next stage in the Hebrew cultural revolution and its success in establishing a cohesive national culture whose members strongly
identified with it at the expense of more personal concerns. The turn to
a plurality of first-person narratives after the establishment of the State,
during what is commonly called the State Generation, marked a break
from the group culture of the first native Israeli generation and a rebellion against it. This book suggests the emergence of yet another cultural
generation in Israel, which, beginning in the early 1990s, can be distinguished by a new voice, the "first person dual" of the romantic couple.
Although the first person dual does not exist as a grammatical category
in Hebrew, the sense of the pronominal narrative voice in many literary
works from that time is neither that of an individual "I" or of a communal "we," but that of the romantic duo ("גוף ראשוניים").

Since Gershon Shaked completed his monumental study of modern
Hebrew literature between 1880 and 1980, few literary historians have attempted to follow his example. The reluctance to do so can be attributed
to a lack of adequate historical perspective, which the proximity to the
new literature bred. Another, more compelling reason, perhaps, may be
related to the arrival of the so-called postmodern age in Israel at the end
of the millennium, an age wary of positivistic studies like those of Shaked,
who based his work and organized it according to his professed attach-
ment to Zionism.[3] Instead of a definitive history, then, the proximity in
time to the literature in question produced numerous studies that focused
primarily on its impressive expansion and diversity,[4] while the attempts to
classify it focused on defining that literature broadly as postmodern.[5]

Since both of these observations about literary diversity and postmodernism are expansive and somewhat vague, I would like to draw in the
following pages a more specific map of Israeli literature during the last
two decades. The chart I suggest here is made more precise by limiting
it to a shorter period of time and focusing on fewer writers. The time I
examine in this book is that between the two Intifadas, 1987 to 2000, and

the writers I consider here are Etgar Keret, Gadi Taub, Uzi Weil, and Gafi Amir. Keenly expressive of the profound changes Israeli society underwent in the last two decades of the twentieth century, these four writers struck a new narrative voice. Instead of the common Zionist "we" of previous generations or the individual "I" who rebelled against it, Keret, Taub, Weil, and Amir adopted an unaffiliated Me and You, an alternative romantic narrative that focuses on coupling and privileges personal love over communal and national attachments.

Characterized by terse narratives that usually unfold in urban settings, the First Person Dual writers seem to have abandoned the grand Zionist story of the past in favor of a narrative that is both smaller and larger in scope—the preoccupation with romantic love as the ultimate fulfillment of the human condition. The works of these writers, unlike those of writers from previous literary generations, appear largely unconcerned with Jewish identity, Jewish nationality, or Jewish history. Moreover, their move away from the particular and the local toward more universal literary themes, and especially the construction of the romantic experience within a capitalist framework, is distinctly marked by the abandonment of the tension between individual and community, a tension that has stood at the center of modern Hebrew literature since its inception. Instead, these writers seek to realize themselves within the confines of a couple rather than in relation to a community.

By the appellation "romance" or "romantic love," which I use freely and expansively throughout this book, I mean the way contemporary culture, as represented especially by the entertainment industry and the mass media, idolizes what it refers to as "true love"—that is, the kind of monogamous coupling based on mutual attraction and sustained by continuous devotion that was first conceived of and popularized during the nineteenth century. Popular phrases such as "soul mate" or "*the one*," which can often be read or heard in many popular movies, mostly Hollywood romantic comedies, capture this sense fairly well. Peculiarly, the liberal sexuality that the mass media reflects and promotes in the West is also accompanied by more conservative "romantic" values that privilege the kind of faithfulness associated more readily with medieval courtship. A good measure of naivety and often even childishness is required to maintain such simplistic idealizations that go against common cultural practices.[6] Guilelessness and innocence, then, whether genuine or contrived, are also part of the way I apply "romantic" in my analysis.

Surprisingly, it is this quality that distinguishes this group of writers and makes them an emblem of a time that was marked by a burst of literary activity and that witnessed the remarkable growth of a variety of distinct literary voices: women, Mizrahim, gays, the religious, Arabs, and others. Throughout the 1990s these writers were mentioned again and again in the daily press as well as in more academic venues, individually and as a group, as the voice of a new Israeli age, an age that is alternatively called postmodern or postzionist. Their resonance in an increasingly fragmented society and the ability of these First Person Dual or romantic writers to reach across a plurality of voices by constructing a fragile but distinct voice is the subject of this book.[7]

This modest study does not purport to be synoptic. At the same time, although it makes no claim to continue the kind of comprehensive classification Shaked offered, it does something similar by different means. The map I chart here suggests the contours of a cultural "age" by presenting a very small but evocative group of writers during a fixed timeframe. With the exception of Etgar Keret, perhaps, the four writers chosen for inspection here were not the most central literary figures of the decade (a decade whose extraordinary literary ferment and diversity makes such determinations very difficult anyway). Various other writers, especially female writers, may have been more visible and prolific. Some were arguably better. Many of them, like Savyon Liebrecht, Dorit Rabinyan, Yael Hadaya, Tzruya Shalev, Leah Aini, and Mira Magen, also privileged romance and eschewed more national concerns. But while their works underscore the premise of this book, they do not present the kind of emblematic similarities that can be more readily gleaned in the works of Etgar Keret, Gadi Taub, Uzi Weil, and Gafi Amir.

The scant attention modern Hebrew works historically gave to romantic love makes the preoccupation of the First Person Dual writers with it especially intriguing. The development of modern literature in Europe, especially the rise of the novel, is directly linked to romance as an individualizing force, a mode of rebellion, liberation, and fulfillment in an increasingly bourgeois, capitalist, and secular world. The very European term for the novel, *román* (from "romance"), makes clear the extent to which the literary form itself centered on relations between the sexes.[8] Generally speaking, this was not the case with modern Hebrew literature, which waged a different cultural war at its beginning and focused more on reforming the Jewish community and forging new connections between its members that were not based on religion. There were, to be sure, genuine attempts to incorporate romance into modern

Hebrew letters. The most obvious example would be the very first modern Hebrew novel, Avraham Mapu's 1853 *Love of Zion* (*Ahavat tzion*). Other notable examples come from the Hebrew Revival at the end of the nineteenth century and beginning of the twentieth (Berdichevsky and Gnessin, for instance). But most of these served more ideological than romantic concerns. While Mapu's novel was a *maskilic* critique of the moribund Jewish community of his day, the precarious freedom that Revivalist heroes won from their traditional Jewish communities often came at the expense of their love lives, which tended to be tortuous and abortive. That is, the failed love affairs of the uprooted young Jew, the *Talush*, were yet another indication of his existential limbo, stuck between the declining old world and an unknown Jewish future.

More contemporary successors of Revivalist writers, the New Wave writers of the 1950s and 1960s in Israel, used romance in similar ways. Amos Oz epitomized this in his signature novel of the period, *Michael sheli* (*My Michael*, 1968), when he endowed the love life of the heroine, Hanna, with distinct national symbolism. The same can be said for New Wave female writers like Yehudit Hendel, Amalia Kahana-Carmon, and Ruth Almog, who, generally speaking, seem more concerned with a feminist agenda than with the potential for romance in their works from that time. The focus of these women writers on physical and psychological interior spaces and on the political dynamics of romantic relationships is especially important for this study because in the long run it legitimized such concerns, leading eventually to the emergence of the romantic writers. This does not mean, of course, that Hebrew literature knew no romance (S. Y. Agnon, for instance). But a comparison to other literatures, certainly English, French, and American literatures, which from the 1960s on exercised a growing influence on Israeli culture, will reveal that romance occupied a secondary role that usually served communal, Jewish, and Zionist politics.

One of the peculiar characteristics of the romantic texts in this book is the recurring urban environments they present, whose setting and imagery often seem taken from generic American films and television programs, including bars, gun-toting detectives, nightly taxi rides in the city, and beautiful, mysterious women. In this "capitalist realism," as Eva Illouz calls it in her illuminating study about the connection between love and modern consumerism, romantic love is perceived as inherently liberating and individualizing, a mode of rebellion, escape, and fulfillment in an increasingly alienating world.[9] It is after all a commonplace that romantic love replaced religion in twentieth-century Western culture and has become one of the most pervasive mythologies of contemporary life in the West. But since nationality, not religion, held center stage in Zionism, the closer identification with the West and the eager adoption of its values, especially love, eventually undermined Israeli nationalism, not Jewish religion.

In Israel, this kind of romantic consumerism occurs most conspicuously in the rebellion of post-army Israeli youth, who take prolonged trips abroad, especially to the Far East. These excursions serve a double purpose. The most obvious one is to disengage physically and mentally from a dismal Israeli reality that is still stuck, as it were, in a primitive and anachronistic conflict while the rest of the civilized world is out having fun. Another purpose is to foster a closer association with the West through the consumption of tailored tours to exotic locations, replete with extreme sports and drug parties that characterize youth culture, especially in Europe.[10] Today we know that these changes were not as enduring, and that in many ways, the economic boom and the chance for peace were artificial. But the fictive quality of both, the economy and the peace, was nevertheless alluring at the time, perhaps even more so because they were an attractive promise.[11] This goes directly to the nature of the romantic writers, who perceived these trends and commented on the possibilities they held for a truly Western, civil society in Israel, an Israel that would finally be able to lead the bourgeois life it always craved.

This, essentially, is the sentiment that the romantic writers express in their works, which usurp the grand Zionist narrative of the past in favor of a more Western-universalist one. While the new narrative retains elements of the former, such as the Arab-Israeli conflict, the Ashkenazi-Mizrahi divide, and secular-religious tensions, these no longer hold the same values they held before. As part of a postmodern, post-national literary universe, they are subsumed under and serve a grander romantic narrative, to which Jewish history, culture, and identity are in many ways incidental.[12]

The study is framed between the two Intifadas because that time saw some of the most portentous changes in recent Israeli history, society, and culture, including the chance for a lasting peace between Israel and its Arab neighbors as well as the country's rapid economic development and its attendant bourgeoisification. At the time, both of these were perceived as having the potential to change the country in profound and unprecedented ways. The discrepancy between the first Intifada, which was perceived by a majority of Israelis as unjust, senseless, and ultimately a losing fight with the Palestinians, and the unprecedented rise in Israelis' own standards of living brought into question the very foundations of Zionism. The second Intifada, however, marked the end to some of these trends because its eruption against the country's protracted economic slump confirmed the intractability of the Arab-Israeli conflict and resurrected Israel's Masada complex. The romantic writers expressed many of the sensibilities—chances as well as dangers—of a new Israeli era after the first Intifada in 1987. The second Intifada in 2000, however, changed this dynamic by eliminating some of the gap that grew between the political and the personal during the 1990s and, harking back to earlier times of national emergency, drew it closer again.

The following four chapters draw a literary map of the last twenty or so years in Israel. The map proposed here focuses primarily on the literature between the two Intifadas as two symbolic milestones that frame the period and inform it. Chapter 1 looks at some of the profound changes brought on by what has been termed the end of the Zionist era during the 1980s. The chapter examines the critique of the old Zionist narrative, often referred to as postzionist criticism, not only by scholars like Benny Morris and Tom Segev, but especially by writers like Meir Shalev, David Grossman, Orly Castel-Bloom, and Yosef Al-Dror, whose diverse works foreshadowed and heralded a new era.

Chapter 2 continues the examination of this new era by focusing on one of its most immediately visible articulations: the growth of a new press in Israel during the last decades of the millennium. The chapter centers primarily on a local Tel-Aviv weekly, *Ha'ir*, which became one of the most articulate voices of a dynamic, urban, and sophisticated young and rebellious Israeli generation between 1985 and 1995. The chapter examines the connections between literature and more popular media like *Ha'ir*, which became a fertile hothouse for most of the writers who are discussed in the next chapters and inspired some of their literary innovations.

Chapter 3 looks at the works of Etgar Keret, one of the best-known and most articulate voices in Israel and abroad, who spoke for a new Israeli generation that no longer abided by many of the old Zionist tenets. The chapter looks at Keret as a representative of an Israeli Generation X, a generation that did not subscribe anymore to many of the old Zionist truisms, refused to sacrifice itself unnecessarily on what it perceived to be a false national altar, and looked for new ways to express and fulfill itself. Chapter 4 looks at three of Keret's contemporaries, Gadi Taub, Uzi Weil, and Gafi Amir, who echo many of Keret's concerns and sensibilities, especially his cultivation of romantic love as an interim solution to the ideological vacuum and confusion of the age.

Finally, the conclusion looks at several works written after the second Intifada in 2000 in order to show how a new generation of young writers returns to some of the old literary paradigms abandoned briefly by the romantic writers. The conclusion makes clear that ultimately, the attempt of the First Person Dual or romantic writers to suggest alternative narratives did not last long. The breaking of the second Intifada silenced their voices and returned many of the old national concerns to center stage. As the new millennium began, the harsh reality of the Middle East announced itself ever more ruthlessly. It erected newer boundaries between Israel and its Arab neighbors, deepened the conflict between them, and returned the old tribalism in more virulent forms.

One   BOURGEOISIFICATION
AND ITS DISCONTENT

I want to draw the emergence of romance in contempo-
rary Israeli culture against a historical moment Gadi Taub describes so
well in his study of a phenomenon he termed the Dispirited Rebellion.[1]
Taub, who is also one of the writers I discuss in this book, published
in 1997 a collection of essays in which he defined a new Israeli generation in what is essentially a post-national era. Taub's thesis is important
for understanding the state of mind of a generation of Israelis who were
born after the triumphant war in 1967 and whose consciousness was
forged in an increasingly safe, economically advantaged, and militarily
strong Israel.[2] The romantic writers are the products of this generation
and, somewhat paradoxically, derive their anxieties from their unprecedented privilege as powerful and secure Jews.[3]

Taub places his discussion of the changes Israeli society and culture
underwent within the larger context of postmodernism—a valuable category for understanding some of the main psychological currents that
shaped the age. The most important element of postmodernism in this
regard is its tendency to bring together disparate elements or ingredients
that do not have an immediate or apparent meaning as a unified whole
(in architecture, literature, music, fashion, etc.). Taub writes that a tendency toward this kind of disconnectedness was one of the most identifying characteristics of his generation. It was an inclination that was
cultivated by the mounting tension between the private and the public
spheres, an increasing pessimism about Israel's political course, a heightened frustration with the ability to change it, and an acute wish to disengage from it in order to protect one's sanity and psychological integrity
in the face of it.

Very early in his book, Taub credits this sense of disconnect to the
first Intifada, the Palestinian popular uprising that broke out in 1987
against Israel's occupation of the territories following the 1967 war. He

writes, "As long as the political problems in Israel had to do with the nation's very existence and Israelis agreed on a common and more or less just way to ensure it, the personal and the communal coexisted well together."[4] But since 1967 this coexistence began to unravel, becoming increasingly uneasy after the 1982 war in Lebanon, and especially after the Intifada in 1987. "A system of values based on secularism and humanism," continues Taub, "cannot support the occupation of another nation beyond a certain point," and a soldier who is required to forcefully maintain this control has to find at some point a rationale for his own behavior and that of his government. If the soldier is not religious, "he must find a political justification for his actions. The search for political rationalization becomes a deep psychological need, more than just an intellectual one so that, suddenly, a lot of weight is placed on the political" (14). Among the most common reactions to this tension was a great wish to disconnect oneself from anything political, a refusal to deal with it, and a tendency to turn away from it and look elsewhere.

The Intifada did not trigger this dynamic as much as it clarified and articulated it for many. The ground for this realization was laid long before the Intifada broke out, not just by the changes in the country's material culture, but especially by so-called new historians and sociologists, whose challenges to well-accepted perceptions of Israeli history gradually entered into academic and then public discourse from the beginning of the 1980s. Studies such as Simha Flapan's 1987 *The Birth of Israel: Myths and Realities*, Benny Morris's 1987 *The Palestinian Refugee Problem*, Ella Shohat's 1989 *Israeli Cinema*, and Tom Segev's 1985 *1949, The First Israelis*, and his 1991 *The Seventh Million*, to name the most prominent of them, began to reexamine some of Zionism's most deep-rooted and hallowed claims about Israel's wish for peace, about its relations with Arabs, about its immigration and social integration policies, and about its relationship to the Holocaust and its survivors. Although these challenges were not immediately accepted and were strongly resisted by the establishment and the culture at large, some of the well-researched and pointedly argued alternative explanations they provided slowly gained credence, especially with younger people. A sense that Israel might not have been right at all times, that it was not always the victim, and that there are other, legitimate, sides to the Middle East story slowly encroached on Zionist dogma.

The first Intifada broke out against this background. And when the country was rallied to fight the Palestinians in the name of some of the tired old slogans about self-defense and existential threats, the call did

Israeli Culture between the Two Intifadas

not ring so true anymore. Moreover, the discrepancy precipitated a cognitive dissonance of national proportions that could not be maintained for long. Taub quotes an angry teenager who had this to say in 1988:

> Life is not what it used to be, on all counts. All the great visions, which in our case means the overused Zionist vision, are preparing us for a vague fulfillment that will never materialize and designate our lives here and now as an interim stage, a state of emergency full of dangers whose end no one can predict. The paranoid assumption, even if true . . . that our proud and small Jewish state is constantly under threat, is used as a shrewd ploy to unite the people and as a wonderful excuse for all the things we ought to have accomplished but never managed to after forty years, five wars and thirty-four records by Hava Alberstein. (19)

This heated but unusual response for the apolitical 1980s ends on a more typical postmodernist note: forty years of Zionist development are dismissed by comparing them with a veteran, folksy singer, Hava Alberstein, ridiculed here for her old-fashioned music and sentimental lyrics from a bygone, gullible era. The majority of young people who were of army age did not actively engage with this tension, certainly not politically. In fact, a sense of disillusion and political disengagement marked the age and distinguished it from past generations. Taub predicates his book on this phenomenon, which he defines by the oxymoron "dispirited rebellion."

In hindsight, hints about the shifting paradigms Taub described in 1997 can already be detected in some of the major literary works that were published almost a decade before that, novels like Meir Shalev's 1988 *Blue Mountain* (*Roman rusi*), David Grossman's 1986 *See Under: Love* (*Ayen erech: ahava*) and especially his 1991 *The Book of Intimate Grammar* (*Sefer hadikduk hapnimi*), Orly Castel-Bloom's 1992 *Dolly City*, and, finally, the scant but extremely influential plays and other writings of Yosef Al-Dror.[5] With the exception of Al-Dror's, all of these were major works, which received wide public attention and marked a discernible change in the self-perception of Israelis.[6]

In its uproarious send-up of Zionism's most cherished myth, the foundational myth of the Second Aliya in the first decades of the twentieth century, Shalev's book exhibits perhaps the most visible change in the attitude toward the grand Zionist narrative, which was inculcated to generations of Israelis from the movement's establishment. The magic-realist novel is an ode to the extraordinary sacrifice of the pioneering men and women who dried swamps, tilled the land, and literally built the country from the ground up with their own hands at a great personal cost. But the half-imagined novel also lays bare the sheer lunacy and folly of some of these pioneers, whose grandchildren fulfill their legacy in highly ironic ways: they profit from their inherited farmland not by continuing to cultivate it but by selling it at exorbitant prices as burial ground for those seeking eternal rest in the shadow of the myth.

The extraordinary success of the novel underscores its importance and reveals something about the profound changes that began to be felt at the time.[7] One of the most remarkable attributes of the work is the lush world of pioneering lore it re-creates, a concoction of foundational stories and legends, slogans, modes of speech, terminology, and other trivia, delivered in an extraordinarily rich Hebrew that creates anew the lofty register of the Zionist founders without sounding archaic. Indeed, the Hebrew of *Blue Mountain*, and of Shalev's oeuvre in general, is perhaps one of the most enduring successes of the Zionist revolution, whose mythological beginnings are "rearranged" in the novel in viciously funny ways.

"One summer night," the novel begins, "the old schoolteacher Ya'akov Pinnes awoke from his sleep with a great start. 'I'm screwing Liberson's granddaughter!' someone had shouted outside."[8] Pinnes is a member of the old Zionist guard, one of the founders of the co-operative settlement that is at the center of the story, a kind of a has-been who still wages fervent battles against breaches in the pioneering protocol years after it has been relaxed, perhaps even abandoned. His very name is a jibe. Pronounced "Penis" in Hebrew, Pinnes is indeed a prick of sorts. "For years," continues the story,

> he had chinked every crack, repaired every rent, stood in
> the breach every time. "Like the Dutch boy plugging the
> dike," he would say as he beat back yet another threat. Fruit
> aphids, state lotteries, cattle ticks, anopheles mosquitoes,
> bands of locusts and jazz musicians swirled around him
> like dark waves before breaking in a slimy froth against the
> breastwork of his heart. (1)

The old-fashioned teacher is clearly regressive. He is a bore and a nag who thinks of himself in heroic terms that sound embarrassingly out of touch with the times ("Like the Dutch boy plugging the dike"). They may have been appropriate once, but they are not so anymore, just as the man himself is not what he used to be. He is old and confused, his hands tremble as he buttons his khaki pants, he needs eyeglasses, and his gait is unsure: "outside he tripped over a molehill subversively dug in the garden" (2). The strict ideological way he perceives the world around him is ridiculed by the amusing mixture of natural and cultural phenomena he fights against. State lotteries and jazz musicians are considered natural disasters like locusts or the mole whose tunnels are dug in a deliberate attempt, as Pinnes thinks of it, to thwart the success of the Zionist pioneering project.

The sexual connotations of Pinnes's name are directly related to the crude and abrupt beginning of the story, which opens with a joyful cry of libidinous abandon. Despite his name, Pinnes is not the one doing the screwing, an irony that is underscored by the fact that he is a childless widower as well. The brazen shout becomes then not only an indictment of the frustrated sexual energy of the pioneers, which could often be diverted and unleashed in twisted ways. The mysterious "degenerate," as Pinnes calls the shouter, literally screws the offspring of these pioneers, or, more figuratively, their legacy. The cry itself, loud, bodacious, utterly reckless and uninhibited, is directly opposed to the ascetic restraint of the pioneers, who purported to dedicate their lives to productive labor in modesty and with few words. It is, of course, ironic that Pinnes should hear the cry, because, as the settlement's educator, the old teacher spent his life preaching the Zionist revolution without really practicing it. At least not with his own two hands, as Zionist dogma dictated. The cry is an ironic mockery of Zionism through a warped mimicry of its rhetoric.

But the remarkable aspect of *Blue Mountain* is not its ironic commentary on Zionism, a tradition that began with the pioneers themselves. The novel is noteworthy for the easy detachment and carelessness with which it regards them. It is not a passionate satire that focuses on the critical difference between an "is" and an "ought," nor a parody that aims to correct a wrong, like most Zionist satires before it. The importance of the book lies in the effortless way it trifles with the pathos of the founding fathers and mothers. Shalev writes with the assurance of a secure and pedigreed son, who looks at his past with ease and good-natured humor padded by the distance of generations. This is the novel's innovation that marks the changing times. *Blue Mountain* is postzionist in the sense that it does not participate in the debates about the value of Zionism that always raged within the movement. The book peers at it from a distance and regards it with a mixture of reverence and amusement. Like the mythological image of Ephraim who walks around in the novel with a giant ox wrapped around his shoulders, the book paradoxically valorizes the pioneers by poking fun at them. The ox is a symbol of the tremendous pioneering feat as well as a grotesque image of its excesses. It elevates and at the same time debunks the grand foundational myth of Zionism as only someone who is very sure of it is able to do.

Grossman's *See Under: Love* foreshadows the new era in different ways that have more to do with the increasing influence of postmodernism at the time. The novel, as its name suggests, is preoccupied with the inherent instability of language as one of the central modes of postmodern critique. Already the title alerts readers to the quality of language as a consciously organized phenomenon whose fluid meaning always needs to be defined and fixed. The sense of linguistic uncertainty and confusion is destabilized further by the quizzical relationship between the "love" of the title and the Holocaust in the book. The tension is upheld throughout the novel, whose four distinct parts wrestle with the need to contain the Holocaust in words and bring what is essentially indescribable under the rule of language. The first part, "Momik," re-creates the novelty and incomprehensibility of the Holocaust by introducing it through the consciousness of a young child whose parents survived the catastrophe. The second part, "Bruno," deals with the Holocaust "linguistically" through silence, by turning one of its victims, the Polish-Jewish writer Bruno Schulz, into a metaphorical fish. The third part, "Wasserman," reverses the utter destruction of European Jewry by introducing a fanciful character who cannot be destroyed no matter how many times he is executed by the Nazis. The fourth part, "The Complete Encyclopedia of Kazik's Life," is a short lexicon that redefines or rearranges real and imaginary events to bestow a measure of grace on the lives of Holocaust victims.

The clue to the novel's linguistic project comes early on, when young Momik tries to understand something about the nature of the Holocaust by looking it up in the Hebrew Encyclopedia.

> Momik loves to hold the big books in his hands, and it makes him feel good all over . . . because who are you, what are you compared to the Encyclopedia, with all the little letters crowded in long, straight columns and mysterious abbreviations like secret signals for a big, strong, silent army boldly marching out to conquer the world, all-knowing, all-righteous . . . and even though he doesn't always understand what they're talking about, he likes to touch the pages and feel deep in his stomach and his heart all the power and

the silence, and the seriousness, and the scientificness that
makes everything so clear and simple. (43–44)

As one of the most ambitious undertakings of the new state, the Hebrew Encyclopedia was meant to lend scientific credence to Zionism.
The nearly thirty-volume work was intended to project the breadth, the
permanency, and the authority of the newly established culture by bring-
ing out a definitive guide to the universe from its perspective, just like
the French and English encyclopedias did when those national cultures
coalesced a hundred or so years before. Momik's sense of comfort and
delight stems from the paternalistic authority of this new guide, whose
words he compares to a conquering army. Coming close on the heels of
the War of Independence, the words of the Encyclopedia thus become a
continuation of the conquest of Canaan by other means, drawing a minute Hebrew map of it and on it and laying claim to it as Israeli.

Yet Momik's praise is ambivalent, and his self-rebuke—"who are you,
what are you compared to the Encyclopedia"—can be construed as critical as well. So is his delight in "the power and the silence . . . that makes
everything so clear and simple." The whole point of the novel is that
nothing is clear or simple about the Holocaust. Momik finds out that
even the Encyclopedia cannot help here. In fact, "there seemed to be
an awful lot of things the Encyclopedia was trying to ignore, as if they
didn't exist" (43). In his childish way, Momik censures the Encyclopedia's authors for their tendentiousness in selecting the entries as well as
for their negligence for not completing the job they have begun (at the
time the story takes place in the 1950s, not all of the volumes had been
published). Read toward the end of the 1980s, Momik's disapproval can
be taken as a general critique of Zionism as dogmatic and incomplete.
See Under: Love undermines this dogma by attempting to complete it in
alternative ways, providing a personal map or guide as a compendium or
even as a replacement for the culture's official manuals.

Grossman's other work, *The Book of Intimate Grammar*, expresses the
passage into a new era in less subtle ways by placing at the center of
the book a protagonist who refuses to grow. Aron, the novel's hero, is a
prepubescent boy who lives in a working-class neighborhood in Jerusalem on the eve of the 1967 war. As imaginative and adventurous as he
is, Aron abhors the repulsive way his friends begin to sprout hair, crack
their voices, and shift their attention from the games and pranks of childhood to girls and sex. He tries to arrest his own maturation by holding
desperately to his boyhood and even invents a present-progressive world,

a linguistic modality that does not exist in Hebrew, by manipulating the English suffix "ing" and affixing it to Hebrew nouns and verbs. Finally, after this inventive stratagem cannot stop the march of time either, Aron climbs into an old, broken refrigerator and locks himself in there in an attempt to freeze himself in time, as it were.

Grossman's wish to arrest time and roll it back is not exactly aimed at the resurrection of a communal coziness of an unspoiled and innocent Israel before the "big bang" of the Six-Day War. The parochial crassness, jingoism, and subdued violence that mark Aron's milieu in the book, which frustrates and depresses him so, is a prediction in hindsight about the eventual outcome of the war. With such coarse and small-minded victors as Aron's parents and their friends, how could it be otherwise? Nevertheless, Grossman's creation of a young hero, precarious, sensitive, and idealistic—an important element that recurs in the works of the romantic writers, especially Keret—is a nostalgic gesture posed as critique. In the last chapter of the book, the imminence of the war and the onset of puberty for Gideon, Aron's best friend, are frantically conflated, sending the desperate hero into a tailspin that eventually lands him in the refrigerator. "Hey, it could start any minute now, today or tomorrow," Gideon says to Aron about the impending war everyone in the country is tensely awaiting. "What could?" asks the agitated Aron, whose mind is fixated on another imminence, the realization that his friend had already passed into the adult world. "Aron shook his head no, he didn't understand, what was Gideon talking about? What did all his words amount to: are you or aren't you?" he thinks to himself, wondering about Gideon's loyalty to him and about puberty. "Aron heaved a sigh of relief, Gideon was talking of nothing but the war. But just when Aron thought he still had a chance, he noticed a dark shadow, new and kinky, where Gideon's thigh met his groin." Aron then demands that Gideon take off his shorts so he can make sure of it, and when Gideon refuses he chases him and forces him to submit. "He stripped the pants off the sobbing youth, pulled them down to his knees. Looked, examined. Then nodded as his eyes began to dim." Aron then leaves Gideon with disgust and disappointment and runs away,

> till at last he arrived and collapsed on the ground, leaning against the refrigerator door. Slowly, as if trying to remember something, he ran a finger up his body . . . investigated his flesh, tracing the geography of the unfamiliar zone of hell. Then he stood up, pulled the cold door handle, opened the

refrigerator . . . folded himself into the lower shelf . . . and looked up at the spangled sky. . . . There in the darkness, beyond the ring of light, he felt the whole nation waiting for the first shot, the great jump-off. Who would win and who would lose? How many would die? (341)

Aron's violent refusal to grow up, poised as it is on the eve of the Six-Day War, highlights some of the more problematic outcomes of that war, which exacerbated the Palestinian refugee problem, escalated the conflict with the Arabs, and deepened the secular-religious divide in Israel following the growth of the settlers' movement. Aron's defiance becomes a rejection of recent Israeli history, and his attempt to cleanse it of contamination is made all the more endearing by its impossibility. The juvenile Aron is a prototype of a protagonist that will appear again in the literature of the romantic writers, mounting a similar critique of the present through nostalgia for the innocence and promise of youth.

In many ways, the works of the next writer, Orly Castel-Bloom, were closer to the literature of the romantic writers than those of Meir Shalev or David Grossman, and foreshadowed it more tangibly. The distinct postmodernist qualities of Castel-Bloom's writing were noticed immediately after her first publication of short stories in 1987, the anthology *Not Far from the City Center* (*Lo rachok mimerkaz ha'ir*), even if they were not labeled as such until a few years later.[9] Almost all readers commented on the strange, discombobulated language of the texts, a pastiche of registers, lexica, modes of speech, etc., that crowd the pages in a dense and frantic disarray. By 1990 most of the critical establishment already declared Castel-Bloom a prominent existential writer, focusing particularly on her style. In an article dedicated almost entirely to Castel-Bloom's language, Dan Miron refutes its definition as thin, meager, or coarse, as has often been suggested, and defines it instead as "tin-like," that is, language that does not try to be mimetic or expressive but focuses instead on its automation, its clichéd quality, the fact that it no longer expresses depth or emotion. Castel-Bloom's stories, writes Miron, "are a cruel parody on the kitschy desire for meaning." The writer, he continues, "rejects any illusion of depth in language, in culture, in the human experience, in the privacy of the human soul, in society, in tradition and in the past." All she sees before her is a reality "made up of a thin and dull layer of automatic and quotidian existence that hides an abyss of chaos below it." [10] Ariel Hirshfeld concurred in his review of Castel-Bloom's first anthology, *Where Am I* (*Hechan ani nimtzet*, 1990), which he saw as a "large and horrifying image of the world as it is imprinted on the soul." The book imparts to the reader "a sense of insult of such vast proportions that it suffuses the world with its shrieking darkness."[11]

Stylistically, then, Castel-Bloom clearly employs postmodernist techniques: language is no longer mimetic but becomes a fetishized medium, senseless, circular, a collection of signifiers without signifieds. Yet, surprisingly, the thrust behind many of these avant-garde texts seems much more conservative. Castel-Bloom's contorted works are primarily allegories of an Israeli world gone bad.[12] As a literary stratagem, writes Ortzion Bartana, Israeli postmodernism "is a satirical-allegorical protest against a harsh reality. The evil and the ugly are embellished in order to be derided and condemned."[13] Many readers agreed that Castel-Bloom's stories are "trapped in a harsh and grating reality, made up from the worst of Israeliana: brutality, violence, detachment," and that they evince the desperation of a dead-end or no-win situation.[14] The pastiche becomes an internal critique "against the oppression of absolute kitsch and the system of values it represents," so that all we can do now "is use kitsch itself as an avant-garde weapon of last resort: the question these days is not how to return to heaven, but how to decorate Hell."[15]

Drawing on this metaphor, Castel-Bloom's first novel, *Dolly City* (1992), is a master class in interior decoration. The novel takes place in an alien, futuristic Israel and tells the strange story of Dr. Dolly, an overly protective mother, whose anxious love for her adopted son almost destroys him. Much of the dense novel is hard to decipher because Castel-Bloom employs here one of her signature postmodern devices. She eliminates the causal connections between syntax and lexicon, between the grammatical propriety of her sentences and the nonsensical or fantastic content or "reality" they describe. The correspondence between the language and what it actually describes exists only on a technical level. The descriptions themselves make little sense. Take for example the opening of the novel, in which the narrator, the bizarre Dr. Dolly, describes the death of her goldfish.

> I took a plastic glass and fished up the corpse. . . . I laid the fish on the black marble counter, took a dagger and began cutting it up . . . until I had turned its body into little strips you could measure in millimeters.
>
> Then I looked at the pieces. In very ancient times, in the land of Canaan, righteous men would sacrifice bigger animals than these to God. When they cut up a lamb, they

would be left with big bloody, significant pieces in their hands, and their covenant would mean something.

I seasoned the strips of goldfish, put a bit on my finger, lit a match and brought the flame up to the flesh of the fish until it was a little charred and my finger too began to smell like a steak. Then I threw my head back, opened my mouth wide, and let the first strip of the fish fall straight into my alimentary canal. (9)

These are all proper sentences that nevertheless make strange sense or no sense at all. The analogy between Abraham's momentous covenant with God (Gen. 15), during which the Land of Israel was bequeathed to him, and the narrator's own absurd mockery of it is even more confounding. Who is this person, readers ask, what on earth is she doing, and why? Some of these questions clear up only after enough obsessive descriptions of this kind accumulate to invoke an exaggerated picture of a deeply sick Israel. The language makes no sense because the society it describes does not. It is a pitiless Israeli society, nasty, mean, lacking in compassion and absent of any vision for a future. What remains of the biblical allusion is its bloody brutality, unmitigated anymore by a redemptive promise or a meaningful narrative.

Castel-Bloom showed an uncanny ability to articulate precisely the inchoate angst of the Israeli bourgeoisie, "to express the emptiness it feels and its inability to define exactly what bothers it behind the comforts of its privileged existence."[16] One of her most important contributions, wrote Ariana Melamed, was the skillful way she mapped the modern soul, delicately, precisely, and subversively, "through the deliberate deconstruction of linguistic and conscious clichés and the paradoxical construction of a nightmarish world made up of the most common and immediate Israeli materials."[17] In various interviews, Orly Castel-Bloom herself acknowledged her agenda, the motives behind her writing. "I ask moral questions; questions about our ability to live in a world like ours. I want to protest, to unite people through some action; I want justice, a sense of brotherhood. I have naïve hopes that I don't think we should give up on. I am an idealist."[18]

These are strange words from the author of such wildly anarchical texts. But this is also the point at which Castel-Bloom adjoins Grossman and makes way for writers like Keret. The value of Castel-Bloom's works resides in the loud cry they raise, a terrible lament of prophetic proportions about the dismal state of the country, its politics, and its culture.

Thus, the very terror that her stories raise becomes one of their most redemptive aspects because it is a terror that expresses an inherent inability to make sense of an Israeli world that lost its anchoring in a grand national narrative; a terror that is both a protest and a call-to-arms of sorts. This is not to say that Castel-Bloom is a reactionary who wishes to reinstate a parochial Zionism, but rather that she expresses a profound sense of loss on the brink of a new era.

Orly Castel-Bloom has often been included as part of a group of writers who have alternatively been labeled Lean Language writers, Postmodernists or Urban writers. Various other names included the Shenkin group and the *mekomon* style of writing. The first name is a reference to Shenkin Street in Tel-Aviv, which in the 1990s came to represent Israel's new urbanism with its artistic boutiques of consumer goods. The second refers to the young writers in *mekomonim,* local weekly papers which the media revolution in the 1980s brought into prominence, especially in Tel-Aviv and Jerusalem, and which were distributed as supplements to major newspapers.[19] Keret, Taub, Weil, and Amir, the writers I call here romantic, were almost always included in that group in one constellation or another. But as I showed in my analysis of Castel-Bloom above, and as I demonstrate with respect to the other four writers later in this book, the work of Orly Castel-Bloom is more meaningful as both a precursor to the urban literature of the 1990s that makes up the major part of this study, and as an overarching influence and reference that frames that period. In terms of scope, depth, and cultural consequence the literature of Castel-Bloom exceeds that of the romantic writers. At the same time, until the second Intifada her frequent publications—between 1987 and 2000 she published nine different works, collections of short stories and novels—continued to articulate her existential terror in similar ways. Keret, Taub, Weil, and Amir, on the other hand, tried to divert attention from these ghosts by suggesting a romantic alternative. Their solution may have been precarious and fleeting, but unlike Castel-Bloom, they still suggested it, which is why I chose to place them at the center of this study.

Yosef Al-Dror is the last forerunner to the romantic writers that I discuss here. Calling him "forerunner" is misguiding, because Al-Dror was not only a peer and contemporary of the four writers; in many ways he founded the group. He worked closely with Keret and Weil on various projects and was a remarkably creative writer who had considerable influence on them. Like Orly Castel-Bloom, Al-Dror returns in his works to the betrayal, the cultural confusion, the helplessness, and the lack of control his generation feels at the brink of a new era. He also tackles these frustrations by manipulating language. But unlike Castel-Bloom, Al-Dror reacts to the confusion and despair not so much by embellishing them as by mocking or disengaging from them through nonsense. In some of his later work he also suggests romance as a vague and noncommittal solution.

Gadi Taub refers frequently to Al-Dror in his study and uses his work as standup comedian and writer for newspapers, television, and stage as some of the most succinctly dispirited expressions of the age. Al-Dror's contributions to two principal venues of the cultural revolution that swept Israel in the late 1980s and throughout the 1990s, the wildly successful local Tel-Aviv weekly *Ha'ir* and the equally popular television skits of the *Chamber Quintet*, were critical in fomenting this revolution.[20] The use of nonsense was one of Al-Dror's most inspiring contributions. First in his standup comedy act in the late 1980s, but more enduringly in his contributions to the wacky *Back Cover* (*Hasha'ar ha'achori*) of *Ha'ir* and then to the *Chamber Quintet* (*Hachamishiya hakamerit*), Al-Dror established nonsense in the English tradition of Monty Python as one of the leading genres of his generation; nonsense with decidedly dark, introspective undertones. During the weekly's heyday, in the first half of the 1990s, its *Back Cover* was the paper's most identifiable feature. For many people it was one of the main reasons they got the paper and the first thing they read in it. A jumbled collection of anecdotes, quotes—real and invented—bits of monologues and dialogues, and flashes of wit, the *Back Cover*, says Al-Dror, "was the best thing that ever happened to me. It was where I was born to myself as a writer. There was no structure, no rules, and the most wonderful thing was that I didn't have to sign my name. Everything was so loose, a sort of a vacuum in which you let language roll freely and bump against itself."[21]

Al-Dror's confession provides a valuable insight into an era that was perhaps frustrating and confusing. But it also opened up great opportunities for a generation that rebelled against its predecessors and discarded its most cherished tenets, without yet having invented new ones of its own. In its wonderfully creative, funny, and iconoclastic jumble of intelligent nonsense, the *Back Cover* was an eloquent expression of the first joy of artistic freedom, imparting a sense of giddiness and weightlessness that comes from unburdening oneself of the past without yet carrying a present.

Here is the August 6, 1993, issue of the *Back Cover*, randomly chosen, which includes the following items: The middle of the page featured a short philosophical musing disguised as drawing-room wit that reads: "Everything has such a multiplicity of meanings these days. People's intentions have become so diverse, so developed and energetic that they have become entities unto themselves. You can frequently see people who have intentions only. There is no personality behind them; behind the intentions, that is. Imagine all those intentions out there by themselves without a person behind them." Next to it we find an absurd, fake ad written in impossible Hebrew that announces: "Due to lack of need of two lines [עקב אי צורך בשני קווים] a telephone line is for sale in the Bialik area of Ramat-Gan for half the price that Bezeq [the phone company] charges (including change of ownership). 5236510." The first item seems like postmodern commentary that contemplates the gap between people's real needs and their imaginary desires in what one assumes to be a world that hurls an endless stream of possibilities or experiences for purchase at them. The second item, while clearly nonsensical and a spoof on similar, more practical ads of this kind, may be a disguised call to slow down, downsize, get rid of an unnecessary plenty that may be ironically contrasted to more dire economic times when Israelis waited years to have a phone line installed but may have been more content with less.

This confusion is echoed in another item in the same column that reads: "Whenever I baby-sit and the baby begins to cry, I am never sure if it's because he needs to poop or because he wants his mommy or something. What do babies like, anyway, tenderness? Violence? Do they like it hard, sweet? I don't know. So I do what always worked for me as a baby—every time it cries, I give the baby a hundred dollars (Tamara Brody, the new girl of the *Back Cover*)." The lack of compassion and connection between the girl and the baby stems not only from the fact that she is a "rented" mother. The girl also talks about the baby using inappropriate and vaguely sexual terminology and highlights the problematic commoditization of love by absurdly trying to soothe it with money. While this ultimate capitalist pacifier is obviously lost on the baby, the girl is likely also chastised for believing in it herself.

Further down the column, there is a disconnected personal appeal that alludes to the romantic narrative: "Aliza, what were we thinking, sleeping in separate beds for two years? Love you, Ron." The *Back Cover* was often filled with similar appeals, usually by men, who crave meaningful and lasting relationships although they seem unable to have them. The appeal here does not specify whether Aliza and Ron have separated as a couple or may still be living together. But the ambiguity is part of the problem that deepens the gap between these two seemingly close people, who are or were separated not only by two beds but by an inability to communicate.

The categorization into genres of the items that filled the *Back Cover* was never clear. Were they ads, announcements, short stories, moralist proverbs, or any other literary classification that comes to mind? Part of their charm, of course, was the inability to label them neatly and their grouping together on one page in a postmodern, nonsensical jumble. The very introduction of "non sense," humor that does not make sense, was groundbreaking in the context of Israel's committed and ideologically mobilized culture.

True, Israel has a long tradition of satirical humor, beginning most famously perhaps with Ephraim Kishon in the 1950s, continuing with the legendary 1974 television program *Head Cleaning* (*Nikuy rosh*) and then the television puppet show *Hachartsoofim* in the mid-1990s, modeled after Britain's *Spitting Image*. But most of these satires and the many others they inspired were politically and socially motivated. True to the genre, their underlying agenda was to reform the country's various ills. Even the successful 1950s and 1960s radio show, *Three in a Boat* (*Shlosha besira achat*), which was nonsensical to a degree, aimed most of all to showcase the country's most famous New Hebrews like a proud parent parading his talented children before the guests.[22]

Al-Dror's humor had none of these attributes. It made few references to politics, local or international, and it did not comment directly on Israeli society, which was a mainstay of Israeli humor as epitomized by the country's longest-running and most successful entertainment trio, *Hagashashim*.[23] Instead, it negotiated the literary worlds of other mostly Western cultures, created its own absurd world in the language, and maintained a tenuous relationship with an identifiable here and now. If it had any agenda at all it was the wish to disengage, to turn away from the social and the political, to be isolated in a virtual world of words whose apparent lack of meaning could not be externally dictated but sprang from the writer's own imagination. In a post-Intifada world in which the traditional distinctions between good and evil, right and wrong, were no longer clear, Al-Dror's nonsense provided not just an outlet but a kind of silent or "dispirited" protest, as Taub would call it. This was no doubt one of the main attractions the *Back Cover* offered: a soothing humor mingled with a peculiarly morbid sensibility whose vague "agenda" seems to have protested the loss of meaning and direction and the abysmal state of the State.

Al-Dror said as much himself. Interviewed in 1993 about his new play *Loop*, in which he honed the kind of nonsense he wrote for the *Back Cover* into sharper and more philosophically poignant meditations, he openly confessed that "there is no generation above us, only a vacuum." [24] The play, he continued, "was born out of a great confusion and is meant to express it. . . . There is a generational disconnect above us . . . who do we look up to, who is supposed to show us the way, who do we learn from? We don't even have a school to rebel against." Confusion seems to plague many of Al-Dror's peers; a sense of loss brought on by the fundamental changes that the country was undergoing then and which were intensified further by the economic plenty and the moral relativism of postmodernism that followed suit. All of this was played out during the first years after the first Intifada. "It was hard during those days," says Amos, one of the characters in *Loop*:

> Psychology was at its peak, and penny-psychology was not even the cheapest thing around. Who would have thought that all the psychologists would be executed? It was difficult in those days, casual sex, casual husband, casual wife, who had a casual baby and raised a casual family. Suddenly, opportunities that came once in a lifetime began returning again and again, more and more opportunities, people buckled under their weight. Everything was possible, everything was allowed. All expectations were met and all hopes materialized, and not in synagogues or in heaven or in faith or in art. On the street, everything happened right on the street, under one's nose, almost inside one's nostrils, if it's possible or acceptable to put it this way, everyone thought that this was *it* or that was *it*.[25]

None of these questions is solved in the play, of course, which rails against the endless stream of false "choices" whose shelf life is as short as the time it takes them to flicker across one's consciousness.

As a writer of absurd plays that rely heavily on language and create their own distinct verbal worlds as part of their message, Al-Dror seems to continue Hanoch Levin's unique theatrical tradition. But the distinct differences between them go to the heart of Al-Dror's role as one of the era's cultural "ideologues." Levin was an intensely political playwright whose plays, absurd as they were, maintained an overt relationship to a concrete Israeli reality which they presented in an almost hyper-realistic manner.[26] This was also true of his singular linguistic style, which relied on the adroit manipulation of different Hebrew (Ashkenazi) argots—social, ethnic, bureaucratic—for its artistic affect. Levin was also a unique and prolific playwright, a "one-man show" who did not inspire a school. Al-Dror, on the other hand, had no commitment to politics in a traditional way, yet despite the limited scope of his output his sensibilities reverberate in many of his contemporaries' works. To paraphrase the essence of the 1990s successful American television show, *Seinfeld*, Al-Dror essentially wrote about nothing. But as with *Seinfeld*, his minute preoccupation with "nothing," with the small absurdities of everyday life that often involve an obsession with words or phrases, examines human relations in a world of shifting and unstable values of gender, race, family, and friendship. Or as Al-Dror himself put it once: "It is becoming gradually apparent that no one has an identity,"

> that is, not while they are engaged in doing something. Identity means consciousness. You know who you are because you and others remember something about yourself, but actually, you are not anything while you are engaged in doing something. I am who I am because my little dog recognizes me.[27]

In an attempt to describe his second and last play to date, *The Obvious (Hamuvan me'elav)*,[28] Al-Dror provides the following summary of the work:

> A salesman of dialogues who believes in ultimate ambivalence meets a messenger who believes in clarity and decisiveness. The messenger, who claims to be sent by Everybody, forbids him to be ambivalent anymore. The salesman appeals the request but is turned down. Two actors who believe in success at all costs join the salesman and argue with him about the perception of reality. One of them leaves while the other stays. An actress, who is tired of being treated as a sexual object, even if it is a legitimate one, approaches them in search of an emotional connection. She also argues with the salesman but at the same time, from the force of habit, carries out a functional relationship with the remaining actor. Between the Messenger, the Woman, the Actor and Ticking Time the Creator's mental condition deteriorates until he achieves a sort of inner peace.[29]

The most fundamental function of language as a system of stable signifiers, a human invention that endows voice utterances or words with mutually agreed-upon values, is questioned here. We understand the word *good* to have several definitive qualities that we perceive as positive, worthy, valuable, and so forth. Even if we deviate from these meanings for various effects, we depend on a common and stable value to produce those effects. One of the most nagging questions Al-Dror asks over and over again in all of his writings is: what happens when these values begin to shift, when some people begin to doubt and question them or replace them with different values of their own?[30] This is very different from Hanoch Levin, whose angry diatribes against the establishment are reformatory in essence and rely on the stability of language for their satirical affect.

The doubts Al-Dror raises about linguistic values express his pessimism about the reality he lives in, his inability to make sense of it, or literally its non sense. Asked what exactly he is accused of, a character called "Creator" in *The Obvious* blames another character called "Citizen" for "emptying words of their meaning, secretly and without permission . . . replacing depth with superficiality and internal with external, deliberately sabotaging the mysterious and the complex, mortally wounding the absurd and the paradoxical, kidnapping terms and selling them on the sly, cultural manipulation . . . severing morality from everyday life and diminishing the ability to tell good from evil."[31] Here, very concisely, we have Al-Dror's complaint about the world and the times in which he lives, as well as his own role as an artist.

Significantly, the characters in the play are not given names. Instead they are called Creator, Citizen, Young Woman, Alef, Bet, and so on. Al-Dror does not think that this makes the characters less human and more symbolic. "It doesn't make them less real," he insists; "this is how people around me speak and behave." But it does give his work a passionate ideological bent. Devising characters who are named after the entity, quality, or trait they represent was one of the hallmarks of medieval literature in Europe, for instance. It marked the ideological intensity of a deeply religious society that put little value in the individual personality of mortals and considered ideas such as God, heaven, and hell far more concrete than the realities of everyday life. In the medieval imagination, spirits and demons were far more real than living men.

Al-Dror's use of a similar device in his play, his engagement with ideas and ideals, seems like a protest against a contemporary culture that falsely claims to believe in individuality and to hold it above all else. This is true especially in Western societies which purport to uphold the belief in the uniqueness of each and every human being and the supreme value of his or her life, but betray it repeatedly in their politics and economics at home and abroad.[32] Al-Dror is not only targeting here a fraudulent secular dogma. He also blames capitalism, which insincerely worships at the altar of an allegedly hallowed individuality. The choices that the forces of the market offer are meant to maximize profits, not to promote equality and compassion, even if they cunningly appear to do so, like Benetton's ads, for instance, and those of countless other retailers. Part of the dynamic created in free-market democracies that promotes this flawed sense of freedom and equality is the exaggerated focus or importance given in its arts and letters to the personal, the individual. The natural course of this historical development in the West, from ideologically symbolic representations in religious art and literature to the increasing concentration on the personal in the novel and beyond, is only part of it.[33] Al-Dror seems to point out that in late capitalism, as the last half of the twentieth century is sometimes called, there seems to be an increasing collusion between politics, economics, and art that is expressed most acutely in an inherent relativism that takes the form of the devaluation of language and the disappearance, diminution, and blurring of ideology as a consequence.

In Israel, the outbreak of the first Intifada brought this process into high relief. The slow erosion of the Zionist pioneering ideals, which is the natural course of any realized ideology, was not accompanied by an equal change in Zionist rhetoric or self-perception. When the Intifada broke out, it acted like a sudden shock that revealed the large gap between words and actions, between the self-righteousness of Zionism, the magnitude of its hyperbole, and its ugly policies toward the Palestinians. Once this disparity was exposed, it was not long before the ethos or ideology itself began to be questioned and then charged for precisely those transgressions the Creator in *The Obvious* enumerates: for "emptying words of their meaning secretly and without permission," for "cultural manipulation," for "severing morality from everyday life," and for "diminishing the ability to tell good from evil."[34]

Perhaps this is the reason behind Al-Dror's insistence on devising a play that refuses to construct verisimilitudes of real people, but instead insists on engaging with ideals on a more pure and rudimentary level as a way to return them to public debate and awareness. The exaggerated focus on the personal rang false for Al-Dror, because, in his experience, opinions of individuals were disregarded in the real world in the same way that individual rights were disrespected and ignored. What Al-Dror seems to be protesting, then, is the way we become victimized by bigger forces that lull us into submission by frivolously bandying about lofty words, words whose real meanings are often discounted.

The disturbing inconsistency that was laid bare during the Intifada between Zionist preaching and practice was further aggravated by the wholesale importation of superficial free-market economic ideals as a kind of substitute for a discarded Zionism. The rapid bourgeoisification of Israeli society during the 1980s and 1990s produced a sense of confidence that had nothing to do with the actual ability of the country to address many of its remaining internal and external problems. The variety made possible by affluence, like the proliferation of consumer goods and services, media venues, and entertainment choices, did not change the makeup of Israel's troubled society and did not take it out of a war-torn Middle East, as much as Israelis wished it or imagined it. "I hate style," says one of the characters in *Loop*, "I hate little sandwiches with Italian dressing, I hate dressings, can't you get it through your head. Do you really think that by eating a baguette for breakfast you internalize Europe?" This was another aspect of a new postmodern, postzionist era that Al-Dror found distressing, the confusion between image and substance, and indeed the frequent mistaking of image for substance, as his musing about the disconnect between people and intentions discussed above makes clear.

Most if not all of Al-Dror's works inherently feed on confusion and add to it or ignore it rather than bring order to a confusing world, as we often expect from art. *Loop*, for example, leaves the characters with neither a solution for nor a hint at the root or cause of their problems. The play, Al-Dror explains, "suffers from the very symptoms it describes" because "it was born out of a deep sense of confusion and aimed to express it."[35] From an artistic point of view, this may be wrong, he admits, because while the artist is expected to bring order to chaos, he, Al-Dror, does not do so in his plays.

But Al-Dror could be selling himself short. His second play, *The Obvious*, which in some ways continues his first play, does suggest a solution of sorts. *Loop* concludes with a reverberating imperative given by the female protagonist to the male protagonist to "go, beat off." In *The Obvious*, the solipsism of masturbation is abandoned in order to explore the possibility of a relationship with another person. The play is a story that begins with a wedding and ends with a partnership or "couplehood" (זוגיות), explains Al-Dror, a difference that is clearly marked by the playwright. In a postmodern era replete with such abundance of symbols, says Al-Dror, many objects and ideas are emptied of their original meaning and begin to function as symbols. Conversely, many meaningful symbols are deprived of their former meaning. Marriage, Al-Dror points out, is one of them. As an institution, marriage has lost a lot of what it meant in the past:

> Creator: In the communication age, from the moment human beings, and especially women, become objects that can be bought and sold, any connection between them will always have the emotional detachment of a commercial act, albeit with some of the excitement that usually accompanies a successful transaction, but nothing more than this, which wreaks havoc on the heart.

At the same time, it also gained a new meaning, glamorous perhaps, but empty.

> Creator: Why have a wedding?
> Citizen: There's an interest to see you married.
> Creator: With her? Why? What for?
> Citizen: For nothing immediate. It's a long-term strategy.
> Creator (bitterly): Yes, I know the strategy.
> Citizen: Some people would consider it as the height of their career.
> Creator: Only people who have a career! (106–107)

The question which the play raises is how clear and how obvious the obvious really is. Getting married in the past was something no one thought too much about. It was an obvious social rite of passage. If you were not married after a certain age, it raised all kinds of suspicions against you and forced you to prove your innocence. "Everyone around you lets out a big sigh of relief after you're married, and that sigh could put out a forest fire," says Al-Dror.[36] The problems start, he continues, once you begin to reevaluate the obvious. "If you use marriage as a way to gain social legitimacy it ceases to be a personal, private affair" and becomes a public performance you put on in order to present yourself to society in a certain way or as a way to fit in.[37] Hence his description of the play as a story that begins with marriage and ends with couple-hood. Al-Dror wants to go beyond the patina of the symbol and perhaps even discard it altogether. He is much more interested in exploring love as a condition of being rather than to engage with its hollow, socially prescribed and sanctioned representation known as "wedding" or "marriage." As they hug and plan a future together, Creator says to Young Woman in the play: "You know, people say that there's a place in Scotland where it's foggy all year round. Wanna go there?" This is by no means a definitive solution to any of the questions Al-Dror raises and which remain unclear, literally enveloped by fog. Significantly, however, Al-Dror does not leave his protagonists to contemplate and confront these questions alone. Their coming together as a couple, isolated so romantically, in fact, in a foggy location in Scotland—and away from Israel—is a solution of sorts. It is not only a respite that suffices for now, but in some ways also an act of rebellion and defiance.

Al-Dror was one of the most incisive commentators of the post-Intifada era, quick to expose its inherent absurdities, keen to treat them artistically, and shrewd to present them in the country's emerging new entertainment venues—standup comedy, urban weeklies (*mekomonim*), and expanded television programming. Paradoxically, however, he was not very visible. He was a standup comic before this imported art form gained wide popularity. He did not sign his name to his contributions to the *Back Cover*. As a writer for the *Chamber Quintet* his name was buried in television credits that rolled by too quickly. His two plays were minor productions that drew a small audience of cognoscenti, and his artistic career seems to have come to a halt with them. Al-Dror was, however, more of a writers' writer, one of those cultural figures whose influence on other artists exceeds in many ways that of their own work. Y. H. Brenner comes to mind in this regard. Many of the more visible "romantics," especially Etgar Keret and Uzi Weil, worked closely with Al-Dror and continued to develop his acute sense of disconnectedness and absurdity, and his preoccupation with meaning in a "meaningless" post-national and postmodern age, in their literary and other works. Significantly, too, they continued to explore his "romantic solution."

Two

POPULAR MEDIA IN
A POST-NATIONAL AGE

Since the romantic writers, like all other writers, were products of their age, I want to consider in this chapter some of the cultural aspects that distinguished the last decade or so of the twentieth century in Israel. Of these changes, one of the most significant was the rise of a new press. The creation and proliferation of new media outlets did not only express and record the profound changes Israel was undergoing. Because the romantic writers participated in these new media early in their careers, their journalistic beginnings render important insights into their more enduring works. This chapter looks closely at one of the most important of these new media, the Tel-Aviv weekly *Ha'ir*. First, because the magazine was prominent. Second, because it was published in and about Tel-Aviv, which, more than any other city in Israel, symbolized the new era. Third, because in the works of the romantic writers, all of whom lived in or around the city, Tel-Aviv is not only the background to their stories. In almost all of them it appears as one of the characters as well.

The emergence of a new press in Israel in the 1980s as an expression of the rapidly changing times has been amply recorded, most comprehensively by Oz Almog in his encyclopedic 2004 *Farewell to Srulik: Changing Values among the Israeli Elite*.[1] The local Tel-Aviv weekly paper *Ha'ir* occupies an important place in Almog's cultural analysis, although it is not the only newspaper he focuses on, of course. Another important bellwether was the daily *Hadashot*, started in 1984 and nicknamed the first "national local paper" (*mekomon artzi*).[2] The daily earned the moniker because it was inspired by the successful local weeklies (*mekomonim*), among them *Ha'ir*, that began four years earlier. Designed as a hybrid between a tabloid and a yuppie magazine, *Hadashot* was, as Almog put it, "a liberal, modern, young, urban, dynamic, witty, provocative, and critical" newspaper, styled after English and American models.[3] As such, and as this long string of adjectives attests, it also meant that it was a "Tel-Aviv" newspaper—a paper which openly and unapologetically viewed the affairs of the country not from some "objective" national perspective as much as from a Tel-Aviv one, from within the Bubble, as the city is often called in Israel, because of its unique and independent nature and its perceived dissociation from the rest of Israeli culture in the way of many cultural urban centers (New York, Paris, Cairo).

In some respects, Tel-Aviv was always a cultural bubble that stood apart from its immediate Israeli environment, a fiercely secular and doggedly hedonistic city, whose denizens saw themselves at one and the same time as Ur Zionists and as citizens of the (Western) world. While ideological and political Israel was fighting for survival, independence, and security—soldiers defended the borders, kibbutzniks made the desert bloom, new immigrants populated new frontier towns—the inhabitants of Tel-Aviv seemed always to be going to the beach, strolling leisurely in the streets, and especially to be drinking coffee, preferably espresso.[4] Or so it seemed to the rest of the country.[5] It was not that Tel-Avivians did not feel part of Israel; they did, but their insistence on leading a normal life in defiance of the country's many abnormalities earned them this reputation. For people who lived outside of Tel-Aviv, this behavior did not seem right somehow. It was also seen as disrespectful of the sacrifices others were making. At the same time, residents of Tel-Aviv considered themselves not only models of normality but also model Zionists. Since one of the most powerful motives that animated early Zionism was to "normalize" Jewish life, Tel-Avivians held on to that creed even if sometimes they had to invent that normality.[6]

During the 1980s, this sense or view gradually gained momentum that was boosted and disseminated by the growth of the local weeklies and the adoption of their "local" sensibilities by national newspapers like *Hadashot*. This does not mean that *Hadashot* was a parochial rag that reported about local, Tel-Aviv matters. The paradigmatic shift it signaled was that, first, the solemn reporting about politics and the supreme affairs of the state, which occupied the media prior to that time, was pushed aside in favor of more immediately sensational news, like crime and human interest stories. Second, having been shifted aside and demoted, the affairs of the state and the conduct of its leaders were subjected to an ever increasing censure by a growing number of critics who adopted a "Tel-Aviv perspective"—that is, a perspective that focused on domestic affairs rather than on security and foreign relations. Many of these domestic affairs consisted of social and economic issues that were neglected during years of Arab-Israeli conflict. They also included a sub-stantial focus on issues relating to the country's developing middle class.

The shift was not only thematic, it was stylistic as well. *Hadashot* distilled many of the journalistic innovations that had been brewing in the media for about a decade before and presented its readers with an admixture of "vulgarity and discernment, highbrow and lowbrow, sensationalism and conservatism, patriotism and criticism, young and old, trivial and important."[7] It was a so-called postmodern concoction that came to define the new media during those years. This was true not just for *Hadashot* but also for local weeklies like *Ha'ir*, which gave a chance to a generation of young journalists, unable to get ahead in the more established national media, to launch their careers. All of the writers or "cultural agents" reviewed in this book were involved in the country's various new media venues in some capacity or another. Etgar Keret wrote film reviews for *Hadashot* and later collaborated with Yosef Al-Dror, Uzi Weil, and others on writing scripts for the wildly successful television show *The Chamber Quintet (Hachamishiya hakamerit)*. Gadi Taub began his media career as a host on a children's television show and then joined the local weekly *Tel-Aviv*. Uzi Weil wrote for *Ha'ir*, and Gafi Amir was a teenage journalist who later also worked for the weekly *Tel-Aviv* and other papers.

The 1987 uprising in the territories, later known as the Intifada, high-lighted many of these innovations because the human and civil-rights dimensions of the popular revolt coincided with a heightened sensitiv-ity to these issues by a maturing Israeli middle class. *Hadashot* was the first paper that recognized it and did not mistake the Palestinian riots in the territories for another Arab war on Israel.[8] Its sympathetic stance toward the Palestinians—in a reversal of traditional roles, the Palestin-ians were seen as a weak David beat up by an unjust Israeli Goliath—was soon adopted by other newspapers. Even *Ha'ir*, which was not concerned with politics in the usual sense, began reporting more frequently about the Intifada—although, following *Hadashot*, and true to its "*local patrio-tisme*," *Ha'ir*'s reporting was even more "parochial," of course. At first, the riots were treated by *Ha'ir* as a curious media event, something that could have been going on in Greenland or Patagonia. It had little, if any, effect on life in the city. But that was precisely the problem. Although the Intifada did not impose any visible disruptions to the city's life, its effect was more psychological, conscientious, or ethical. The longer the uprising dragged on and the greater the misery of Palestinians became, the less viable it was to stay morally unimplicated in what was going on in the territories, especially for the denizens of Tel-Aviv, who were doing so well.

As a local paper, *Ha'ir* had an approach and a commitment to politics that were naturally different from those of the national papers, all the more so since it was not the local paper of just any old city, but *the* paper of *the* Israeli city, Tel-Aviv. *Ha'ir* promoted first and foremost not just a new civil society but also a new consumerist society. Most of its pages were dedicated to raising readers' awareness about their various municipal and civic rights and to discovering new consumer products and new ways to consume them: foods, restaurants, clothes, décor. These were very welcome breaths of fresh air, which the residents of the city relished. Finally, they felt, the rest of the country was catching up with them. After almost fifty wrenching years of conflict and strife, it was legitimate, natural, even commendable, to cultivate "a measure of natural and comfortable permissiveness devoid of any hang-ups," as the clever and acerbic columnist Doron Rosenblum put it.[9]

Doron Rosenblum, together with several other distinct commentators who wrote in *Ha'ir*, most notably Eli Mohar, came to define the ascendancy of a new bourgeois culture. This was a culture, as Rosenblum so succinctly put it, which could finally take pleasure in the little joys of life. There was much Rosenblum made fun of in *Ha'ir*'s obsessive navel-gazing and its penchant for fantasy and self-aggrandizement. "Immediately after it first appeared," he wrote in an article commemorating the *mekomon*'s fifth anniversary, *Ha'ir* "pounced with the verve of immigrants from other cities on the invention of a gigantic Tel-Aviv, metropolitan, artistic; a city of sins and theaters, a local Manhattan or a petit Paris."[10] From its first day, continued Rosenblum, *Ha'ir* was extremely meticulous in its conceptual invention of a "Tel-Aviv,"

> The paper began counting, sometimes with too much gravity, the buttons and knots in every notions store; it marked the number of sesame seeds on every bagel and gave them names; it reviewed with the thrill of a museum critic shop after shop, curlicue after parapet, [artisan] cheese rack after [homemade] pickle rack, and did not forget to comment on the last one-eyed cat.

Whether invented or not, the new dynamic took hold until, finally, it was not possible anymore to distinguish between what was authentic and what was merely a pretension, wrote Rosenblum. "Words propped the city up. Tel-Aviv really became colorful and diverse, happy, self-aware, and full of options." If reality sometimes did not live up to its description in the weekly's pages, that was its own fault, not *Ha'ir's*, wrote Rosenblum. It made no difference anymore whether the myriad of entertainment spots and the instant celebrities were created first on paper or vice versa. Both existed in mutual dependency.

But Rosenblum did not only criticize. He found much to celebrate in these new and exciting developments:

> *Ha'ir* . . . [is such] a pleasant habit. . . . It is part of the weekend routine and a central part of the Tel-Aviv invention itself. . . . In its first five years this paper . . . has brought the spring to Tel-Aviv in the dead of summer: a bit of intimacy, a certain weekend joy. *It doesn't slake a thirst as much as it articulates the hunger of an entire generation: an appetite for silence, for individuality, for nonsense, for bagatelles, for peace, for simple weekend calm, for the small pleasures of body and soul, for a measure of indulgence and silliness, for the humdrum of a tranquil town, for small pleasures,* . . . for the invention of culture and all those other pieces that make up the very big thing called normalcy. (My emphasis.)

If, wrote Rosenblum, normalcy will not come from above, maybe it will rise from the bottom. If political change will not hasten its arrival, maybe the decision of a no-name gallery owner to declare himself a masterpiece will bring it about. And it must have worked, Rosenblum concludes his review, because "Tel-Aviv has bought all of the wistful fibs about itself, lock stock and barrel."

His critical conclusion notwithstanding, Rosenblum was clearly proud of his newly discovered city and especially of *Ha'ir*, its leading voice. From a journalistic standpoint, he asserted, "it would be hard to exaggerate the importance of the historic breakthrough that the weekly made," which was first and foremost a generational revolution. This is something Oz Almog points to as well.[11] *Ha'ir* and other young papers like it enabled a generation of Israelis who were born with the State or a little later to express themselves publicly and independently for the first time. Until the weekly and other papers like it came along, public opinion was shaped primarily by old-guard newsmen and -women, representatives of what Rosenblum calls a stagnant Zionist establishment that still had a hold on politics and on the country's veteran news media. Since the young guard could not push the old aside, they overtook them altogether by establishing new venues that gave voice to what Rosenblum describes as "the urban, dynamic and confused Israeli reality."

The term *confused* is important here, especially since the exact word Rosenblum uses, נבוך, includes a sense of hesitancy and embarrassment that is central to the writings of Keret, Taub, Weil, and Amir. It stands in contrast to the conviction and certainty that characterized the older generation, which by the 1980s turned into what Rosenblum calls stagnant. Perhaps, he muses, the energy that was poured into art and into journalistic enterprises—verbal creations rather than more tangible ones—was a reaction against a moribund and corrupt political system, a system that seemed resistant to any real change and forced an exasperated new intelligentsia to focus on the everyday instead of on politics. Whatever it was, Rosenblum points out that *Ha'ir* blazed a trail. It abandoned national and political matters and instead focused more locally and individually, inspiring many papers to follow suit. So new and so refreshing were these local weeklies that "they are the first sections you pull out of the pile of weekend papers," wrote Rosenblum in a resounding testimonial.

Eli Mohar was another important contributor to *Ha'ir*, part of its cadre of urban commentators. In 1984 he began writing a running commentary for the weekly made up of his observations about little details or episodes from the city's daily life, something like the *New York Times's* Monday section, "Metropolitan Diary." Mohar was born in Tel-Aviv in 1948 and lived in the city all his life. Before he began writing for the weekly, he was known as a popular song writer. Maybe because he was older than most of the weekly's other contributors, he chose to give his column a somewhat old-fashioned, even nostalgic name: "Some Goings On in Our City" (*mehana'aseh be'irenu*). In the preface to an anthology of these commentaries, published in 1994, Mohar explains that he chose the old-fashioned title in order to balance some of the weekly's trendier proclivities, especially its penchant for slang and hyper-current Hebrew.[12]

Whether he meant it or not, Mohar's name for his column brings almost immediately to mind one of the first and certainly the most memorable and celebrated collections of local Tel-Aviv lore, Nahum Gutman's anthology of early Tel-Aviviana, *A Little City and Few Men within It* (*Ir ktana ve'anashim ba me'at*).[13] Gutman, who immigrated to Palestine in 1905 at the age of seven and settled in the first neighborhood of what later became Tel-Aviv, has drawn the city's image in its infancy more palpably than any other of its early residents. In his ink sketches and short, anecdotal stories, Gutman—later one of Israel's celebrated painters—recorded small details and random episodes from the city's early life: the first classical music concert, various human types like the town doctor, various neighbors, and physical objects that made up the town's urban landscape, like its first streetlight, gardens, houses, trees.

Mohar's choice, if he indeed named his column as a tribute to Gutman, seems strange at first. Gutman's stories conjure up a small, quiet town, quintessentially parochial, familiar, friendly, and naïve. The Tel-Aviv of *Ha'ir* was a different city altogether; it was gigantic, metropolitan, artistic, sinful, as Rosenblum wrote, a local Manhattan or Paris. There seems little connection between the two cities, separated by more than sixty years. Moreover, part of the charm in Gutman's stories comes from their novelty and from their sincere sense of wonder and pride about the town's many "firsts": its first concert, its first streetlight. Gutman was a good storyteller, but his stories about the beginnings of Tel-Aviv transcended their literary charm. Tel-Aviv was not just the pride and joy of its first residents, it was also the pride and joy of Zionism, the first and only originally and truly Jewish city in the Land of Israel, a symbol of the daring and vision of the Jewish national enterprise.[14]

Age must have had something to do with Mohar's nostalgia, which in turn may have been related to his childhood, passed in a much smaller and less urban Tel-Aviv. But there was something more than that, not just in the name he chose for his column but also in the kind of column it was. Mohar was not simply hankering after the proverbial good old times, not even symbolically or metaphorically. What he was trying to resurrect in his column about Tel-Aviv was the wholesome nineteenth-century bourgeois ethics it once possessed. One of the most endearing aspects of Gutman's stories is the stability, kindness, and civility that the early burghers of Tel-Aviv seem to project. Theirs was an orderly society that derived its strength, its security, and its sense of worth from a meticulous attention to details: the distance between the houses, the amount of space dedicated to gardens, the exact hours for the afternoon siesta, and the kinds of activities permitted and prohibited during it.[15] In short, a peaceful society that constantly works to improve the quality of its citizens' lives.

This is precisely what Eli Mohar set out to do as well. "On these pages," he stated in one of his early columns, which he quotes verbatim in the preface to his anthology,

> a dogged attempt is usually made to stick to those little
> things which in other places make up what people casually
> call "life" (it was like that here too once): different trees, dog

owners (and their pets), someone's laughter, a sunny street corner, the fetching gait of a certain lady, the smell of fried meat patties that fills the vestibule, the neighbor across the way.

Later in the preface he confessed having felt progressively guilty about his persistent praising of the most trivial things. "Do they still exist?" he quotes Nathan Alterman's poem "Yareyach" (Moon), "May I whisper to them 'Hello'?" More than nostalgia for old Tel-Aviv, Mohar tried to renew in his columns the attention to life's little details, to those baga-telles that give cities their character, that make them both unique and timeless. Here was the specific connection to the spirit of Gutman—the quest for normalcy. After years of strife and conflict, Mohar and others like him, at *Ha'ir* and elsewhere, relished the opportunity to revive some of the early sensibilities of Zionism, a Zionism that predated the conflict with the Arabs, a Zionism that was earnestly engaged in normalizing Jewish life and making it quite literally uneventful and peaceful.

Alterman's poem, which Mohar refers to, calls up this very sensa-tion. "Even an old view or prospect has a moment of rebirth," begins the poem by the most Tel-Avivian of poets, a poem about the comfort and delight in familiar, old things: clear sky, a moon atop a cypress tree, the smoothness of water, the stillness of the night. After decades of disrup-tion, Mohar is delighted to resume some of Gutman's simple pleasures, his quiet basking in the humdrum of the everyday. The pleasure both Gutman and Mohar feel comes from the volatile, insane background against which both carve out a niche for sanity and normalcy. They may be separated by more than half a century, but they are united by simi-lar sensibilities. It is true that Gutman's delight in the quotidian derives from its innovation, from the fact that the first streetlight in Tel-Aviv had, in fact, historical implications as a tangible proof of Jewish national independence. Mohar's commentaries, on the other hand, derive their significance not from their innovation as much as from the proof they provide for the endurance of Gutman's spirit, which captured the begin-ning of normal Jewish life decades earlier.

Here, for example, is Mohar's panegyric to an automatic teller ma-chine, an ATM, which echoes Gutman's words of wonder about the city's first streetlight. Taking a late-night stroll in the dark streets of the city, Mohar writes: "Nordau Boulevard is dark, and so is Ben-Yehuda Street, and only the distant faint light that shines from the wall is soothing."[16] It is the light of "our friend the ATM." "Aside from light and warmth," admires Mohar, "the ATM provides us with interest and suspense, like a public gambling box: will it grant your wishes quickly with a reassuring hum, or perhaps stop for a long while in contemplation, as if evaluating you and then refuse to hand you back your lovely card?" Gutman sounds very much the same when he writes about the first streetlight of Tel-Aviv seventy years earlier, about the "green light that spread throughout the small lantern . . . a goblet of greenish light that shone on the circle of onlookers who blinked their eyes, as if surprised at a birthday gift. A reassuring and delightful light. Your ears became accustomed to the hum [of the lamp] . . . which lent the street a special, constant tune, a tune we shall call civilization, which set its foot in this quiet place and stayed with us."[17]

Both writers do not just marvel at a technical innovation. They celebrate a proof of their own civilization, a life of security and comfort. The streetlight and the ATM mark their progression and their roots, a little detail that makes up their life in all of its simplicity, but also in its permanency and stability and in its future promise. Gutman's streetlight marks a line in the sand between the troubled Jewish past and the promise of a much better future. Mohar's ATM picks up where Gutman left off by shifting the focus once again to what Rosenblum defined so eloquently before as "an appetite for silence, for individuality, for nonsense, for bagatelles, for peace, for simple weekend calm, for the small pleasures of body and soul, etc."

Mohar, of course, does not live anymore in a sweet little Garden City, the Tel-Aviv of yore. Although he writes of the city's trees, its changing seasons, its little old ladies and its other human fauna, he also records the march of time, its progression from a dinky frontier town to the Western metropolis it is or would like to be. In a thoroughly amusing column from December 15, 1989, titled "Extra Curricular Courses in Givʿatayim" (חוגים בגבעתיים), he notes some of the city's more radical signs of progress.[18] "A few weeks ago," he begins, "I saw in the personals section of [Haʿir] a charming announcement that made me pause with respect and appreciation for its author,

> and I hasten to commend it because unlike other personal
> ads, shorter in scope, self-interested, petit bourgeois and
> almost small-minded in the simplicity of their desire, here
> was a grand and sweeping ad that can certainly be said to
> have vision. The ad announced simply (and humbly in
> my opinion) that—"a man is organizing a group [חוג] for

submissive women and dominatrixes in Givʻatayim." That
was all. My first gut reaction was—how nice. An extra-
curricular course or a club is something very pleasant, cul-
tured, different. And reading the modest, restrained words
I felt that here was an entrepreneur whose hand I'd like to
shake. For what do we have here if not a sweeping optimism,
a wish to do great things, and a dream, a grand vision. There
was, it seems, a certain man in Givʻatayim, an ordinary
neighbor, who sees himself as an organizer, a guide of sorts,
who fancies not just one or two ladies of either kind but a
whole group, a veritable club, an adult ed facility.

Mohar clearly makes fun of the ad as well as of his own old-fashioned
sensibilities. But he also marvels at the progressiveness of his fellow residents, and especially about the fact that they feel so comfortable expressing their, well, "different" sexuality in the open. The very fact that they
even have this kink means in some way that they have finally arrived, that
they have "made it," as the saying goes. People under stress, whose lives
are in danger, who fight for survival and live in strife or penury, have little
energy and time for these kinds of luxuries. Deviant or alternative sexuality is after all an indication of a highly civilized society, some would even
say decadent, a society which has stabilized and secured the lives of its
citizens and freed them to pursue their happiness in any way they want.
I am not saying, of course, that "deviant" sexuality is the mark or essence
of progress and civilization, only that it is usually found in highly sophisticated, urban, and affluent societies whose members have the leisure and
means to pursue it. Very likely, this is some of what Mohar is admiring
about the ad and why he describes it with a touch of grand, Zionist flair.

"For what do we have here," he gushes about the ad, using language
that is usually reserved for expressing lofty ideals or for penning Zionist
panegyrics, "if not a sweeping optimism that knows no bounds, a wish
to do great things, and a dream, a grand vision." To the Israeli ear, this
language resonates with a myriad of Zionist inspirational expressions,
in speeches, songs, slogans, and posters.[19] But Mohar elevates his language even further when he describes the "grand vision" in the poetic
language of the Bible. Where is this vision taking place, he asks? "In the
clefts of the rock, in the covert of the cliff (בחגוי הסלע, בסתר המדרגה), that
is, in Givʻatayim." His use of the searing poetry of the Song of Songs
(2:14) is reminiscent of a device Zionist propaganda frequently used in
its public relations campaigns. Slogans like "with one of his hands he

is doing work, and with the other he is holding his weapon" (מחזקת השלח באחת ידו עושה במלאכה ואחת, Neh. 4:11) to describe the efforts of the pioneers to develop the land and defend it at the same time were ubiquitous.[20] The choice of Song of Songs is ironic, of course, since Mohar uses its exalted love poetry to describe a kinky sex club. At the same time, the irony is not entirely complete. The connection between the Zionist pathos and Mohar's bathos is the pride and enthusiasm with the national project. Sexual "depravity" may not usually be a cause for celebration. But when it denotes security, affluence, and leisure for a society that was established with the expressed intention of achieving these very goals, it *can* be laudable.

A more subtle commentary on this paradoxical combination is the subject of Mohar's February 23, 1990, entry called "Nineveh, Nineveh," a reference to the sinful city in the book of Jonah, doomed by God for destruction because of the wickedness of its people. Sitting in the plush seat of a taxi on his way to *Ha'ir's* editorial office, his weekly column in hand, Mohar looks out at the passing streets of his city, feeling comfortable and important, "a little like a government minister at work." This reminds him of the frequent sightings in Tel-Aviv of high officials traveling to and fro in their limos, scrutinizing important documents, speaking gravely on the phone, "perhaps even with the prime minister." As a child, he himself saw Ben-Gurion traveling in his car many times, although "I don't remember seeing him looking at papers during the ride, it seemed as if he usually looked out . . . at the city lights, at people, at the cafés, the shop windows, . . . at the blinking of the movie theaters' neon lights."

Some people say, he continues, that the bustling sights of the indulgent city, a stark contrast to his beloved "chilly Negev nights, silent and lofty," would make Ben-Gurion sigh sadly and mutter, "Nineveh, Nineveh." For Mohar, however, this is not a disparaging epithet but rather one that fills him with pride. "I sat back in my seat," he continues,

> and read my document with leisure and felt uncommonly
> at ease . . . like a minister or a prime minister (and maybe
> even senior officials at the European parliament in
> Brussels). . . . I was silent and concentrated, at my best,
> occasionally lifting my eyes up from the paper and glancing
> at the street outside. All was well. Life went orderly on.
> Passersby went on their way, stopping sometimes to look
> at one of the shops. It was one of those rare, ordinary days
> when the earth does not split open, no bus is blown up, no

party convention is being held; everyone goes about their business. The city looked almost innocent, carrying absent-mindedly on, as it were, and it was almost impossible not to appreciate it a little from the depth of the cushy softness and the bright silence of the cab. To keep it a little on its toes, I shuffled my papers and muttered with a nod of my head, as befits my position: Nineveh, Nineveh. But I wasn't really angry.

What Ben-Gurion saw as decadence perhaps, a divergence from Zionist ideology and asceticism, Mohar regards as the very fulfillment of that dream. Here was his city, an ordinary sort of place, peaceful and relaxed, where everyone could go about their business with ease and confidence, to window shop, to sit at a café and drink espresso, to stroll along the streets at night and marvel at ATMs or even organize sexually titillating activities. The reference to Brussels is not accidental. Mohar frequently invokes Europe as a point of comparison. Not just because Europe has been part of Israel's DNA from its inception—its founders all came from its eastern parts and built the country to a large degree in its image. Mohar also looks to Europe as the epitome of an old and civilized society, thoroughly bourgeois, privileged enough to enable its members to pursue their individual happiness in peace.

Ha'ir was all about these sensibilities which Rosenblum and Mohar expressed with such pointed humor. The entire paper waged a spirited civic society campaign aimed at turning Tel-Aviv, and, it hoped, the rest of Israel, into a bourgeois haven. In many ways this was a radical agenda, since *bourgeois* was one of the worst epithets in the Zionist arsenal. To be called *bourjuoy*, Russian for "bourgeois," was a grave insult to a pioneer, a discredit to the fervent socialism of the Zionist revolution. And although that revolution died many years before, and socialism has long lost its hold over the country, its legacy was never flouted with so much moxie.[21] While a great proportion of Israelis were always *bourjuoys*, the power of a Zionist establishment that professed otherwise held public acknowledgment and displays of it in check. But when that power waned and its media became obsolete, latent bourgeois tendencies surfaced, stoked by new venues like *Ha'ir*, which dedicated a great deal of energy to marketing ideas, products, itself. The new city of Tel-Aviv may have been an invention, the product of a public relations or a marketing campaign, but as Rosenblum had noted, "words propped the city up"; the virtual reality eventually materialized.

Ha'ir invented a kind of poetics of consumerism that informed every aspect of the paper, from the actual consumer goods it promoted of lifestyle, dress, food, and leisure, to civil rights, civic involvement, environmental issues, and even religion and politics. The paper was designed to its last inch, not so much graphically as linguistically. If the new Tel-Aviv was a copywriter's invention, *Ha'ir* could have been the industry's trade magazine. The way Almog defined the writing style of *Hadashot*—liberal, modern, young, urban, dynamic, witty, provocative, and critical—can easily be attributed to *Ha'ir*, which extended it even further. No topic was beyond the editors' witty, creative, and acerbic pens, as this random collection of headlines can attest (most of them lose some of their poignancy in English):

- "Air[acist]-Conditioners" (נְזְעָנֵי אֲוִיר), about discrimination against Arabs in Israeli sky clubs, August 22, 1986, p. 19.
- "One Thousand Brides for Five Grooms" (כלות לחמישה חתנים אלף), a takeoff on the famous 1954 film *Seven Brides for Seven Brothers* that deals with power peddling during coalition building after the national election, Aug. 22, 1986, p. 29.
- "Hail Caesar, We Who Are about to Die Salute You" (ההולכים למות מברכים אותך, קיסר), punning on the gladiators' salute to the emperor Claudius before going into the deadly arena that deals with the head of the labor unions, Yisrael Keisar, whose last name is the Hebrew pronunciation of "Caesar," Nov. 28, 1986, p. 19.
- "Thus Shall Be Done to the Man" (כְּכָה יֵעָשֶׂה לָאִישׁ), a partial quote from the book of Esther (6:11) about her uncle Mordecai's preferential treatment by the king. The quote is ironic, because the article deals with the prosecution of a man who broke into the women-only section of the religious beach in Tel-Aviv, Sep. 4, 1987, p. 11.
- "Down with Blacks" (הלאה השחורים!), a mock-racist headline of a cosmetics article about treatment of blackheads on the skin, Oct. 7, 1988.

In a way, the topic became secondary to the way it was presented or phrased. The paper gave style a high premium and often covered issues from what appeared like a detached angle that considered its representational aspects as much if not more than its substantive ones.

Gadi Taub dedicated a chapter in his *Dispirited Rebellion* to what he termed "The Dictatorship of the Pose," by which he meant style.[22] Taub understood the normalizing value of putting style over content at a specific historical moment. The cultivation of style can be important, he writes, especially when an entire generation attempts to shake off "the deadly seriousness, the choking sense of an ever-present danger, and the militarism" of old Israel: "An entire generation decided it wanted to be happy, to go to clubs, to write about indulgence, to pierce its navel, to strike a pose . . . because the besieged collective and the constant invocation to serve the nation prevented the cultivation of intimacy and individuality."[23]

But Taub also warns that, although the wish to be normal was important and healthy, it had risks, namely the dangerous blurring of distinctions, and the loss of a clear system of values. Gal Uchovsky, who was one of *Ha'ir*'s most important cultural critics and briefly edited the weekly in the early 1990s, concurred.[24] The new weeklies may have created a virtual universe that was disconnected from Israeli reality; they refrained from staking their own positions, and preferred nonsense to matters of importance, even when they wrote about them. But, he maintained, their innovations contributed much more than the simple sum of them. Their iconoclasm changed Israeli society profoundly by making it more civic-minded and more democratic.

Every item in the weekly was calculated to create this impression and especially to map in detail the emerging, new world of opportunities that was coming into being in Tel-Aviv. Large sections of the paper were dedicated to minute reporting and reviews of new lifestyle venues like music, restaurants, shops, parties, and other leisure activities. Editions often had detailed guides or maps to the proliferating consumer scenes the city offered, like "The Tel-Aviv Meat Map" (July 15, 1988) about the best places in the city to eat meat, or "The Great Humus Excursion," a comprehensive guide to the city's humus eateries (February 7, 1990). Many of these new places were not only reported, they were reviewed as well with the seriousness that was reserved in the past for matters of national importance. "To my amazement," writes food critic and later restaurateur, Erez Komarovsky, "a fillet steak that I ordered arrived cut up into thin slices that were beaten to death. The lamb chops, succulent but too spicy, deepened my disappointment tenfold." In language that combines the sensationalism of a news story with a poetic register, Komarovsky reports about a . . . steak.

This was not unusual at all. In fact, for a time, authors and poets like Amnon Zhakont, Ofra Riesenfeld, and Hezy Leskly used their poetic gifts to describe consumer goods, which they routinely reviewed in the substantial space the paper dedicated to it. A new aftershave reminded poet Hezy Leskly of "an airport in the West / neat and efficient / neon lights mixed with the breath (הבל פה) of air-conditioning."[25] At the time, these products meant much more than the simple objects that they were. To many Israelis they literally represented opportunity and choice. They meant a closer connection to the rest of the world, particularly the West, about which Leskly clearly rhapsodizes. The poet chooses an airport, a transportation hub that connotes movement and freedom, and focuses on its steady brightness, the cool air that circulates within. The Hebrew term he uses, הבל פה, translated as "breath" here, connotes the power of words to instantly conjure up a world, a vision (להקים/לבנות בהבל פה). It is a slight vision, no doubt, that can just as easily disappear, but for a moment it can be powerful, transporting the aftershave users from a warm, humid, and disorderly Israel to a brighter, cooler, and tidier universe.

Film and television commercials, an emerging industry at the time, also made their way into the review columns and were treated as if they were artistic creations, like films. On August 9, 1991, for instance, on page 72, the well-known commercial for the chocolate yogurt product, Milky, was given detailed credits, including director: Dan Shilon, cinematography: David Gurfinkel, creative directors: David Tamir, Orit Ringel, Yig'al Shilon, Score: Koby Oshrat, Producer: Anat Oz, art direction: Eitan Levy, as well as participants: Helly Goldenberg and Aviva Paz. I mentioned the names of the contributors because some of them were bona fide artists, known for their contributions to more legitimate artistic endeavors. Dan Shilon was a well-known TV producer, director, and host. David Gurfinkel was a leading film director of photography, and Koby Oshrat was a known composer of Israeli popular songs. With time, this kind of critical attention subsided, but when commercials first began to appear on Israeli TV after the mass communication deregulation in the early 1990s they were a novelty, and an admired one at that. It was a sign that verified for many people the country's capitalist Westernization, both aspects of which, capitalism and the West, were eagerly embraced.

A review of the new double-decker buses that were put into service in the Tel-Aviv–Jerusalem line in 1990 illuminates the public's excitement with consumer goods and the platform *Ha'ir* gave it. In a short piece titled, "It Was Superb, Travel Impressions from a Trip to Jerusalem on a Double-Decker Bus," Yo'av Eldad writes: "[This bus] is one of those small big things, that corporate bodies like [the bus company] Egged usually don't consider important. If I were not tethered to my house, I would live on this bus. It sounds like a jet and smells like a train, it has killer air-conditioning, four video screens and the seats are (very) comfortable."[26] The trip between Tel-Aviv and Jerusalem is a short forty-five-minute commute. For the reviewer, however, it is an exciting and impressive excursion that warrants a "travelogue." The bus connotes another world, a glimpse into the plush comforts most Israelis at the time saw only in the movies or in Europe or North America, if they traveled there. In 1990, Egged was still a big, national bus company, against which the small man, that is, the reviewer, positions himself as if it were "the establishment." It is no longer sufficient for the bus company merely to convey people between points. In Israel's emerging consumer economy, they must do so comfortably as well. What the reviewer seems to be saying, then, is *caveat venditor*—that is, let the seller, not the buyer, beware.

Another lively part of the paper that created a veritable urban community was its classified section, called קחתן, translated as "Give-and-take" in the sense of negotiation. Like many of the paper's other parts, this was more than merely a commercial or consumer section. Comprising exchange and bartering as well as buying and selling, the section charted the emerging young urban community that was taking shape in Tel-Aviv. In addition to offering traditional categories like housing and cars, *Ha'ir*'s classifieds also functioned like a community bulletin board and included more personal categories like messages, greetings, classes, and sales of various items. These may have long been integral parts of newspapers elsewhere in the world, but they were not so Israel until that time. In a country of modest means, few and small urban communities, and an obsession with existential politics, they were negligible parts of the media until then. In its characteristic enthusiasm and wit, *Ha'ir* gave the various classified categories quirky names: the housing columns were called Roof, the car columns were called Wheels, and the personals section was given the cheeky label Boys and Girls.

The "Give-and-take" classifieds probably contributed more than any other section in the paper to the creation of Tel-Aviv's imagined urban community, a virtual community that quickly became real. That the value of the classifieds section extended beyond the immediate utility of its various items was clear from the fact that it was one of the paper's most popular sections, second only, perhaps, to its "funny pages," the *Back Cover.* "Newspapers have all kinds of ads and announcements," wrote

Eli Mohar in one of his weekly columns, "of which the well-loved 'Give-and-take' was known from the first day of *Ha'ir* for being dynamic and straightforward, and which, aside from its stated utilitarian purpose, was also regarded as legitimate reading material. This was, I believe, a novelty indeed that made it unique among classified sections in other papers."[27] Mohar identifies the reason for the section's popularity when he writes,

> one of my favorite expressions, probably because of its rug-ged military associations that conceal a hidden tenderness, is the popular phrase "keep in touch," [a classified category] which all kinds of fair, ponytailed young women, who trav-eled on the number 61 bus last Friday when it rained, use to connect with the guy who was wearing a black jacket who sat behind them and definitely looked at them. I like this "keep in touch" so much that I never skip any of its ads. With stubborn optimism I carefully check each one to see if perhaps one of those young women is looking to connect with the pleasant, cool oldster who walked down Nordau [Blvd.] looking all around him with hope . . .

The existence of a section like "Give-and-take" and especially the cat-egory Mohar admires was a testament to the growing size of the urban community, whose members began to suffer some of the attendant con-sequences of the City's growth: alienation and anonymity. At the same time, Mohar's commentary illustrates some of the positive reactions to these trends, namely the development of alternative levels of intimacy that are suited for the new situation and turn the city into a small village again. In a way, the intimacy between the ponytailed woman and the black-jacketed man extends now to the entire city, which is privy to their burgeoning romance.

"Give-and-take" also included a personals section, which, according to Mohar again, was "truly a novelty among the classifieds at that time." These were not the kind of ads put out by matchmaking services that were usually geared toward older people who wanted to settle down and marry. The novelty was that many of the ads were for casual sex and meant to serve the city's growing young, single population.[28] Including the personal ads as part of a more commercial section of the paper was not a comment on the value or practice of sex as a commodity. It was not only an expression of the metropolitanization of Tel-Aviv, whose young men and women, like those in other central cities in the West, met in bars, restaurants, and in the city's other proliferating gathering places.

It was also a testament to the centrality and dynamism of the classified section, which acted as a virtual community center. This is why it was not only "legitimate reading material," as Mohar called it, but one of the most widely read sections in *Ha'ir*.

An even newer element within the personals section of "Give-and-take" was the inclusion of gay and lesbian ads, something truly novel. Gay personal ads appeared before that time, but they were relegated to the few and meager publications that were targeted directly at gays, like Israel's longest-running gay magazine, *Maga'im* (1987–1995).[29] *Ha'ir*'s breakthrough was to casually include ads by gays and lesbians as part of its general personals, which were divided into four categories: Boys, Girls, Boys/Boys, and Girls/Girls. The decision to do so highlighted the different nature of the section and the paper at large, the fact that it was geared toward young people who wanted to have fun. It also gave the paper a genuine urban cachet. The flowering of a homosexual subculture often attended the rise of cities and in fact signaled it, because the survival of a gay subculture usually depended on the size, the anonymity, the variety, and the tolerance that only a sophisticated urban community could provide.[30] The gay and lesbian section in *Ha'ir* was one of the clearest indications of all of these trends which "Give-and-take" reflected.

Ha'ir did not relegate gay issues to personals only, but often raised them openly in various articles as part of its more general campaign to raise civil and civic awareness. One example that iconoclastically combines the two is a titillating article about gay cruising during the Yishuv period.[31] Instead of focusing on some of the sober issues that are commonly associated with that time of national anxiety and peril, the article discussed the cruising habits of gays then: "The main meeting point was below the London Garden [by the beach], on the esplanade and in the garden's bathroom. A row of British soldiers and officers would stand there waiting in the bushes with their members hanging out." The paper ignores the dramatic and heroic aura that the period is usually accorded by exposing some of its more personal elements. Apparently, some men also had time to have a little fun between their brave fighting for the country and their resistance to the British who occupied it.

Early on, *Ha'ir* recognized that the gay presence in the city was numerically substantial and important also as a creative force and as a pool of discerning consumers. A number of later prominent gay and lesbian artists, journalists, and cultural figures were among the paper's earliest and important contributors, including poet Hezy Leskly, cultural critic Gal Uchovsky, who edited the paper in the early 1990s, and journalist, feminist pundit, and author Orna Kazin. The high profile of gays and gay issues in the weekly was a general indication of the paper's cultural politics, as was its focus on Arab and Palestinian civil rights, but it was also a sign of the genuine urban culture that was developing in Tel-Aviv.[32]

The discussion of gay issues was only part of the particular attention the weekly gave to civil rights in general, of which the cultivation of secularism figured prominently. During 1993, the paper began a series of investigations into what it called "religious coercion." Titled "The Secular Are Waking Up" (מרימים ראש), the column recorded various abuses of Israel's religious administration, the Chief Rabbinate, and other instances where the secular population is required to subject itself to religious law.[33] Criticisms of the religious establishment in Israel were raised before this time. But *Ha'ir* raised the volume as well as the urgency of this kind of critique. In doing so it was emboldened by the creation of a Labor-led, Left-leaning government as well as by a sense that the impending peace accords with the Palestinians would weaken the hold religious parties had on the political process in Israel and enable, finally, the development of a normal, Western-like liberal society.

Some of its more sophisticated critique of religious-cultural politics, however, was subtle, like Orna Kazin's amusing guide on how to conduct a proper Yom Kippur.[34] The pugilistic defender of women and gay rights enumerates in the article what readers would need in order to have a traditionally kosher Yom Kippur. "Let's say that you'd like to do it right this year, by the book, to fast properly, go to synagogue, be on good terms with God. Not for any special reason, just for a change. Here are some things you'll need to buy." The guide is actually a critique of religious practice. It has nothing to do with religious belief or spirituality and everything to do with a consumed experience, as the advertising argot it adopts makes clear. The assumption it begins with—"let's say you'd like to do it right this year"—is ludicrous from a religious standpoint, which mandates strict adherence to ritual, especially during this most holy of holy days. If readers still do not get it, Kazin goes on to emphasize the experience as "just for the hell of it." Her final reassurance as to the quickness and ease of achieving the experience is that all you need is a list of products available for sale. Whether Kazin meant to mock belief itself or just the hypocrisy of those who profess it is less important than the flagrant nature of the critique itself.[35] As part of its civic campaign, *Ha'ir* saw no role for religion in the public sphere.

The paper also had plenty of sections devoted to detailed items that dealt with various aspects of city life, including ordinances and regulations, legal issues, and even the court system. All of these had their news value, of course, and the paper often covered them because they affected the city's residents. But *Ha'ir* also wanted to educate its readers about the more fundamental aspects of these affairs as the infrastructure of a democratic society and as a way to strengthen its backbone, a robust middle class. When on October 30, 1987, the paper launched a new section called "The Courthouse" (*Bet hamishpat*), the intention was not to provide sensational crime stories but to educate readers about proper legal procedures. Ostensibly small and insignificant, "The Courthouse" and other sections like it were part of its campaign to raise awareness for individual and civic rights. Grandly speaking, the column was another sign for the erosion of Zionist communalism, its privatization, and its delivery into the hands of individual Israeli citizens, who instead of waiting for the state to take care of them began to do so themselves.

Ha'ir functioned as a practical handbook for this process. Even its lighter sections that dealt with consumption of various goods, venues, and leisure-time can be considered parts of this guide for the rising, urban middle class. They did not simply encourage consumption but also educated the public on how to do so. Since the variety and number of products and pastimes that began to be available to a growing number of people were relatively new, *Ha'ir* mapped them out first and then showed the public what to do with them, how, where, and when. A section like "Bizbuzim," for example, which literally means "spending or wasting [money]," did just that. On the day it debuted, June 12, 1986, it advised readers on designing their wedding, on choosing a portable bidet, on distinguishing gourmet cheeses, and on selecting decorative stones for their gardens. All of these are products for conspicuous consumption that no one really needs. But they indicated the existence of wealth, the wish to dispose of it, and the availability of experts who advised readers how to do so.

The political aspect of *Ha'ir*'s focus on consumption and its use to advance a cultural agenda that went beyond simple profit can probably not get any more obvious than on the day "Bizbuzim" published a detailed financial guide to immigration from . . . Israel! "Every once in a while," began the column on December 28, 1990, "the question comes up whether the time to immigrate has not finally come." After this outrageous beginning, writer Shahar Bar-On goes on to offer sensibly and in a businesslike fashion what he called "advice for families without too much money but with a lot of self-respect, [all] legally and according to proper procedures." It seems almost redundant to mention the disdain

with which Israelis who left the country to settle elsewhere have traditionally met, even in the relatively relaxed 1990s. Israeli Hebrew coined a
special word for it, *yerida*, meaning descent, decline, or fall (from grace).
Hebrew already had a specialized word for Jewish immigration to Israel,
the positive *aliyah*, meaning ascent. *Yerida* was minted as its opposite,
reaching its lowest negative connotation with Premier Yitzhak Rabin's
infamous 1970s description of Israelis who left the country as a "fallout
of weaklings" (נְפוֹלֶת שֶׁל נְמוּשׁוֹת).

Moreover, the fact that the article was published during the beginning of one of the largest immigration waves in Israel's history, the influx
of nearly one million Jews from the former Soviet Union, highlights its
political aspects. It was as if *Ha'ir* was saying that nothing should be kept
off the table, that any topic is legitimate for discussion, and that there are
no taboos, or sacred cows, as Israelis like to call them. What made the
article even more provocative was that it did not even debate the mer-
its of the issue, but presented it as a straightforward consumer item. It
would be simpleminded to suppose that *Ha'ir* truly saw it as such a matter of fact. It did not. But by taking the sting out of it in advance and presenting it as a financial not an ideological issue, the paper made a very
clear political statement. In some ways it was a very patriotic statement
too. Not the kind of jingoism which is usually mistaken for patriotism,
but a thoughtful and educated comment that was aimed at strengthen-
ing the democratic nature of the country and the civic and civil rights of
its individual citizens. Immigration, the article was saying, should ultimately boil down to a personal choice based on comparative assessment.
A government who really treated it as such would perhaps care more
about its citizens. Such government would compete for its citizens by actually improving their conditions of life rather than rely on a tribal sense
of commitment or exterior threats to unite them.

It is not surprising that a few years later the paper published an amusing article on some of the consequences of this trend. In a parody of sorts
of old Zionist rhetoric the article, titled "A Tel-Aviv Boy," reveals how the
typical Tel-Aviv teenager "doesn't like the rugged outdoors, and values
shopping more than a hike in the wild. He is alert, quick to spot new
trends, and has no desire to lead."[36] Although the article is ambivalent
about the value of these priorities, it still spoofs the kind of gushing praise
that was ubiquitous during the early stages of Zionism. The rhetoric that
Zionist ideologues used to announce the creation of a new kind of mas-
culine Jewishness in Israel usually emphasized ruggedness, forthright-
ness, and love of nature, which were cultivated in juxtaposition to an

allegedly effete Diaspora Judaism.[37] The article reverses all of these back again. It does not present young Tel-Avivians as effete, but it certainly points to a radical change in their system of values, which "reflect their parents' desires. This is a consumer generation," the writer continues, "the children internalize their parents' behavior: they eat out, watch lots of entertainment shows, and shop."[38]

By pitting the two images against each other, the old and the new Zionism, the writer critiques the trend, but there is also a measure of admiration in her description of it as the sign of a new era. Like many of the items published by *Ha'ir* during its heyday, this was an iconoclastic article as well. It took an old, accepted Zionist ideal, tenet, belief, or premise, aired it, and examined it anew, exposing the discrepancy between the origin and its status in the present. The writer of the article, Harpaz, does not criticize either type directly, neither the New Hebrew of the past nor its contemporary offspring. She points to the difference between official rhetoric and the new cultural facts on the ground, a shift in values that has occurred over time, and which the public may not have realized or internalized yet. At its best, *Ha'ir* provided readers with such refined and entertaining skepticism that was aimed at revamping the culture and overhauling it.

Some of the old guard regarded *Ha'ir*'s tough consumerism, its attention to civics, and its acerbic reporting style, which informed its more direct political coverage as well, as a pose, the silly, irresponsible antics of an indulgent generation, "tempted by all kinds of mannerisms . . . without realizing that it is missing an opportunity to make a real difference." While the rest of the country was busy with serious issues like politics, economics, and the Intifada, *Ha'ir* and its like "tediously gazed at their own navel, listed the pubs in Tel-Aviv, compared the quality of snacks in its various kiosks, and worked hard to produce false cultural icons," wrote Gideon Sammet in *Ha'aretz*.[39] It would be hard to find a better example of what Taub calls "the choking sense of deadly seriousness" that characterized the older media in Israel.[40]

This is what *Ha'ir* had to say about it. Marking its 500th issue, the paper supplied the following raison d'être for the anniversary:

> It is not a good idea for a paper that tries to be independent, wise, smart, good-looking, tall, wealthy and an expert in pasta to make mistakes of this kind. Still, even *Ha'ir* has fallen into the trap it was always aware of and decided to document itself. And, as always, it immediately qualifies itself,

Israeli Culture between the Two Intifadas

raises an eyebrow and explains with relative charm that it is
not really part of it all. So long, and thanks for all the fish.[41]

Here, in a nutshell, is the weekly's editorial philosophy: independence,
iconoclasm, a sense of humor, irony, self-doubt, but also egotism, smug-
ness, detachment, and above all style. Even if the novelty of each of these
components, as well as their powerful combination, eventually wore
out, they earned the paper an iconic status during its first decade.[42] The
frivolous and unabashed self-praise was refreshing in the sombre media
scene of the 1980s, especially since it stood in contrast to traditional Zionist traits that were increasingly perceived as false. In the past, praise
was lavished on the state, on its society at large, on its achievements, and
especially on its army. It was not used so blatantly for self-promotion.
Moreover, the Israeli penchant for directness and bluntness is taken here
to extremes when the paper disqualifies itself before it even states anything. Finally, the sense of detachment is maintained throughout, not
just detachment "from it all" but from its own self as well. At the same
time, the paper's aloofness receives a mischievous twist when it places
its detachment as a standard, as a contemporary Guide to the Perplexed
(מורה נבוכים), by quoting from the *Hitchhiker's Guide to the Galaxy*—"so
long and thanks for all the fish"—a book that achieved iconic status at
the time among young Israelis as a sort of guide to contemporary life.
We, the paper says, are not part of any of this at all. We hover above it,
looking down at it over our glasses like a privileged sage.

One of *Ha'ir's* most important contributions, then, was the breaking
of that monolithic monopole and the introduction of different perspectives, mostly through iconoclastic humor. For a number of years, the
style which Sammet was so appalled by functioned as content as well.
The so-called navel-gazing may have been indulgent to a point but it
also introduced an alternative angle that did not exist before. By doing
so it literally supplied the public with another choice, to use consumer
terminology. More important, that additional choice eventually affected
the older media and especially their cozy relationship with the establishment, making newspapers in general better in many ways.[43]

The vantage point of the Tel-Aviv bubble made it possible for *Ha'ir*
to be a serial killer of "sacred cows," the biggest of which was Israel's
conflict with the Arabs and the IDF (Israeli Defense Forces), both of
which were untouchable until then by the popular press.[44] Even before
the Intifada, the paper published what would have previously been considered shocking, outrageous, even blasphemous references to the IDF.

In a 1986 article titled "Legends of the Past, Friends" (האגדות שהיו, רעי), Hana Kim challenges some of the culture's most cherished beliefs about Israeli military superiority over Arab armies.[45] The Hebrew of her title is a parody of a famous 1956 victory song called "Facing Mount Sinai." The first stanza of the popular song is, "No, it is not a legend, friends / nor a passing dream / here on Mt. Sinai / the bush still burns / it burns in song / on the lips of our young regiments / and the City's gates / are captured by the Samsonites." The references in the song are to the capture of the Sinai Peninsula in the Sinai Campaign. But whereas the song magnifies the legendary dimension of the military operation through biblical references and by insisting that the stupendous achievement is real, not imaginary, Hana Kim reverses its meaning in her article by questioning some of the most celebrated stories about the IDF and the real value of some of its operations. Many of them, she writes, were legends indeed, fabricated stories based on half-truths.

Another, more quintessentially iconoclastic, article can be found in the September 13, 1991, issue of the weekly, which lists famous Israeli failures or fiascoes. The fact that the paper mentioned the failed battle for Mount Hermon in 1973 was not so unusual anymore. By this time readers of *Ha'ir* were getting used to such iconoclasms, especially with respect to the army, which the weekly almost hounded. The new aspect of the article was in the fact that it listed military debacles side by side with very different kinds of flops in a jumbled concoction. Following the military defeat, the writer lists a failed ad campaign for Kinley soda, as well as the writer's personal failure to become a sex symbol. The unusual combination itself flattens distinctions, if not in the name of postmodernism, then in order to underline the paper's defiant civic agenda.

Some other stone-throwing articles worthy of mention include the bursting of the Masada myth, the exposure of the cult of bereavement, and the many scathing articles about Israeli aggression toward Palestinians during the Intifada.[46] "Attention, Masada Is Falling," declares an article that exposes the creation of the Masada myth and its metamorphosis into one of Israel's most cherished historical events.[47] "I am definitely interested in spoiling that myth," says geographer Sefy Ben-Yosef. "Why should the act of fanatics that ended in cold-blooded slaughter be an example for noble national ethics?" he asks. Another article, whose long name says it all, reads "The Celebrities of Bereavement—They Lost Their Sons [in war] and Became Sought-after Public Figures. The Rating of Bereavement Is Higher than Ever."[48]

Of the many issues connected with the IDF, bereavement was probably the most sensitive because it did not deal directly with the army but with the families of soldiers who died in service. Because of the emotional and deadly nature of the conflict with the Arabs, parents of fallen soldiers were respected as the ultimate contributors to it, sacrificing their children for the safety and security of the nation. But as the blind trust in the army's command and its proper use by politicians eroded (especially after the first Intifada and thanks in part to *Ha'ir*'s exposure of these shortcomings), even that last hold, bereavement, or more precisely its sanctimonious treatment by the media, was questioned. One of the most devastating attacks on it was penned by Uzi Weil in the *Back Cover*:

> —"Ma'am, I am from [the daily] *Yediot Aharonot*, you are
> a bereaved mother, your son fell [in the line of duty], I'm
> not leaving here until you tell me something special and
> interesting about him."
> —"He was boring," she admitted and wiped a tear, "I listened to him once by mistake and fell asleep."
> —"Impossible," I yelled at her, "try. Make an effort. You're a
> bereaved mother, for God's sake."

When the reporter comes back to the office empty-handed, his editor yells at him:

> —"Do you want to keep your job?" the editor frowned at me.
> —"I do, I do . . ."
> —"Then get it through your head," he cut me, "boring people die in nursing homes! . . . I am giving you a last chance," he yelled and slammed on the desk a note with a name and a telephone number. "Here's another mother, bereaved five minutes ago. Go get something out of her that I can put on the first page!"
> —I left. I knocked silently on the door. I went in. I gave my condolences. Discreetly, I asked for a moment of her time, I know it's hard, but now more than ever, so that the nation would know what kind of men give their lives for it night and day, a few words only that describe what kind of a person he was.
> —"No problem," said the bereaved, "first of all I want to say that my son was a homo."
> —"I beg your pardon?"

—"Homosexual. You know, prefers his own sex. A fag, as they say."

—"Yes, but . . ."

—"And it's such a shame that he died just now," she added, "because he only came out of the closet a month ago."

—"Oh."

—"Yes, he and his company commander."

—"His . . . ?

—"His company commander. They both went to the Chief of Staff and asked to be recognized as a couple."

—"The Chief of Staff?"

—"Discreetly, of course. The Chief of Staff said no problem and they drank a toast and then the Chief of Staff asked my son to give him a blowjob. He was really stressed, there was a big drill that day. In the south. All he wanted was to relax a bit."

—"The Chief of Staff?"

—"Yes, yes, the Chief of Staff."

—"Of the IDF?"

—"My son refused, of course."

—"Well, of course."

—"He wasn't into older men."

—"I see."

—"More into children."

—"I see," I said and wondered whether there was a job for me in the local weeklies.[49]

The excerpt needs little explanation, especially the heavy-handed fun it pokes at the media's cynical sensationalism. But it also targets the sanctification of bereavement in the culture at large, something which was more novel, daring and rare. The piece completely desanctifies the soldier's death by making him human, an ordinary person like any other whose death does not elevate him in any way to quasi-sainthood. The first dead soldier is not only ordinary but a colossal bore as well. The second soldier's imperfection is not only his homosexuality but especially his pedophilia. Their faults are exaggerated as a way to resize dead soldiers to their human dimension as well as to counter the culture's inclination to glorify them. Such glorification, the piece seems to be saying, can be a dangerously addictive habit that compensates for a more direct engagement with the reason for those deaths in the first place. Perhaps they were not even justified. If both soldiers and their families would treat these deaths as a terrible tragedy that may have been prevented, other options beside the military one could conceivably be cultivated to deal with Israel's Arab neighbors. The piece comes close to comparing the Israeli cult of fallen soldiers to radical Islam's culture of martyrdom represented by the *shahid*.

But it was the Intifada which attracted *Ha'ir's* most consistent political attention and its harshest, most acerbic criticism. Since the ongoing rebellion in the occupied territories was never perceived as a fight for life or death, the establishment's harsh treatment of the Palestinians was perceived as unjust fairly early on. More important, the clashes in the territories were judged by *Ha'ir* first and foremost from a human-rights perspective, not from a military perspective or from a historical angle that saw it as part of the Arab aggression toward Israel in general. This was, again, new. In part, this attitude stemmed from the fact that when the Intifada broke out Palestinians had already been integrated into Israel's life and especially its economy for decades. Israelis were used to their proximity, and many were personally acquainted with them. The rise in the standards of living of Israelis and the development of civic awareness also contributed to the resentment which members of the country's growing middle class felt toward the early attempts to crush the rebellion, indicated sharply by the then minister of defense Yitzhak Rabin's instructions to the IDF to "break their bones."

Journalists like Gideon Sammet scoffed at *Ha'ir's* fluffiness and its preoccupation with nonsense, "while the rest of the country was worried about serious issues like . . . the Intifada." But he was wrong. Not only was *Ha'ir* energetically engaged in promoting an important cultural revolution. It contributed to the national debate over the Intifada by applying to it its new civic standards. One example of many is a column by *Ha'ir's* architectural critic, Esther Zandberg, from February 12, 1988, titled: "The Density—1730 per Square Kilometer" (*Hatzfifut: 1730 lekamar*) (15). Zandberg launched a column in *Ha'ir* that was one of the first to raise readers' awareness of their urban environment, leading to the conservation of landmark buildings, and to preserving the city's architectural legacy and integrity. In this particular entry she applied her professional standards to a political situation. She did not comment directly on the conflict with the Palestinians. She illustrated how bad the situation was in the territories by talking about population density. Zandberg did not use grand arguments from the old Zionist arsenal. She used a civic argument that appealed to her readers' own bourgeois sense of comfort and environmental awareness. Ostensibly, the point she made was specious, because she did not talk about urban neighborhoods but about refugee camps, which are crowded spaces by definition. But by doing so she humanized the Palestinians, stressed the unfairness of the situation, and argued for their right to have a better life as well.

Other references to the Intifada were more politically direct and unsqueamishly critical of the state as well. On the first Yom Kippur after the Intifada began, *Ha'ir* dedicated its cover to a paraphrase of the holy day's prayer of *Ashamnu* (we are guilty) that amounted to a scathing confession of the country's collective guilt in oppressing the Palestinians. Instead of the usual litany of trespasses Jews recite on Yom Kippur as an act of contrition, the September 16, 1988, cover alluded directly to the Intifada and began: היכינו, הרסנו. . . טרינספרנו, אטמנו, בעטנו, גירשנו, דכאנו, meaning respectively, "we sealed [houses], we beat up, we expelled [Palestinians], we oppressed, we transferred." The prayer continued:

> we shot, we handcuffed, we came down hard, we embittered, we clubbed, we sealed, we pulled out an eye, we blew up, we censured, we buried, we were wicked, we defaced, we abominated, we went wrong, we deceived. For all these, O Lord, we ask for your forgiveness—what do you want from our lives? We were not guilty, we felt no shame, we did not stammer, we shed no tears, we felt no remorse, we couldn't care less. Conclusion (חתימה), and that's it.

The most telling aspect of this blatant confession of guilt is its total dismissal at the end and the shocking disregard for it. As bad as the litany of crimes is, the failure to take note of them is far worse, according to the cover. We may publicly wring our hands about it, but no one truly cares—a far more serious transgression.

Inside, the edition also included an insert for the holy day, a mock Monopoly board called "Intifada" (pp. 78–79), which had categories like roadblocks and other obstacles (Palestinian) players must pass through. Some of the cards players receive with assignments on them read:

- You need a Bibi.[50] Wait three months until the curfew is over.
- Proceed to detention.[51] You'll receive an explanation later.
- Support your brothers' efforts. You're stuck for 4 rounds without [your car] tires.
- Change your identity card. Go to the military administration building and wait 13 rounds.

- The hunting season has started. Hide under the board until game is over.
- Get a ticket to the Allenby Bridge.[52] Take your family and leave the game.
- You were exposed as a collaborator. Hang yourself.
- A bulldozer covered you in sand.[53] Pay 200 for your rescue by the military administration.
- You sabotaged IDF property. Pay a fine of 500.[54]

It was not *Ha'ir*'s criticism of the Intifada that finally convinced the government to make an about-face and change its approach toward the Palestinians. The signing of the Oslo Accords in 1993 and Israel's recognition of the Palestinians' right of self-determination were not the paper's doing. The paper was only a bellwether of currents that ran much deeper. It expressed a widening sense of tedium with the shrillness of old Zionism and its grandstanding. *Ha'ir*'s popularity made clear that the public was ready to move on, to finally put to rest the prolonged and debilitating animosity toward the Arabs and pick up again the civic agenda that was all but abandoned shortly before the Six-Day War. Economic improvement was only part of it. Other changes, that began after the 1973 war, came to fruition during the 1980s, among them a growing sense of skepticism about the country's leadership and the consequent opening up of the culture to more diverse voices and reference points, including Mizrahi, religious, gay, etc., that competed for attention.

As the historic peace accords with the Palestinians drew closer, the paper became increasingly giddy. From 1992 until the assassination of premier Yitzhak Rabin in 1995 the light of Oslo illuminated many of its articles, which took these positive signs as a surety and considered peace not just with the Palestinians but with the rest of the Arab world as inevitable and imminent. Issue after issue brimmed with articles that celebrated the arrival of a peace to end all wars. Judging from those articles, it was as if the entire country sighed deeply in relief that it could finally come out of its mental bunker and enjoy not just a newly found freedom after the siege has been lifted, but also a warm welcome from the family of nations which shunned it for so many years. Not just from the Arab world, which was opening commercial and diplomatic offices in Israel, but especially from the West, toward which most Israelis looked for example and approval.

Many of those articles were not directly about the peace negotiations. A majority of them promoted civic issues aggressively and attempted to discredit blatant expressions of nationalism, which the paper considered jingoistic. Skepticism about the army was only a small part of it, with articles announcing the refusal of reserve soldiers to serve in the Gaza strip,[55] unabashedly explaining why Israel lost in the Intifada,[56] and openly reporting how being discharged from service for psychological reasons is not shameful anymore but in fact turning out to be legitimate and even "cool."[57] Other articles promoted civil rights by examining Israel's own shortcomings with respect to the treatment of its Arab citizens and Muslim culture in general. An Arab reporter, Haled Sa'ad, wrote an article about discrimination in the workplace, and compared his treatment by potential employers before the Oslo Accords and after them.[58] A job he applied for unsuccessfully before Oslo was suddenly available to him after the accords were signed. Another article, "A Good Mosque Is a Dead Mosque," was an exposé of Israel's sanctimonious complaint about Jordanian abuse of Jewish holy places. The report reveals how in Israel, abandoned mosques were turned into restaurants, discotheques, and lottery stations.[59]

The discrediting of some of the country's most ingrained national symbols and institutions was another expression of the winds of change. On August 21, 1992 (21), Ran Reznik reported on plans to cancel the playing of the national anthem, Hatikvah, at the end of the day's broadcasts. The format—a closeup of the national flag billowing in the wind to the sound of the national anthem—had been set from the beginning of television broadcasting in Israel in 1968. It was now slated to be discontinued. An article undermining the vaunted internal security forces, the SHABAK, was less symbolic perhaps but a much sharper indication of the changing times. Titled "Sadists in State Service," it describes the interrogation methods of alleged terrorists by the institution's agents as torture.[60] Care for civil rights took precedence in the article over issues of security, which until that time were paramount in the minds of Israelis, who ignored repeated violations of individuals' rights to protect the country from what were perceived as greater dangers.

Other articles amounted to what was later labeled postzionism, the critical academic examination of some of the country's accepted conventions, old ways, old truths, or old narratives. Such for example was an article questioning the wisdom of maintaining the Jewish National Fund.[61] A venerable body that raised funds to purchase land in Palestine and later Israel and prepare it for Jewish settlement, the institution may have outlived its usefulness, claimed the article, not least because it discriminates against Arabs who cannot take advantage of its various projects. A more comprehensive critique in that vein was Elly Hirsch's review of a new Jewish historical atlas.[62] "After years of MAPAI tyranny," writes Hirsch, who liked the atlas very much, "and the slow annexation by MAFDAL, the freed Zionism of MERETZ shines forth with its renewed emphasis on knowledge and erudition." MAPAI was the early incarnation of the Labor party and held the reins of power during Israel's first twenty-nine years. Its historical conduct came under increasing critique in the 1980s and beyond as having been crude and aggressive, especially with respect to Israel's Arab neighbors and the absorption of Jewish immigrants who came from those countries. The national religious party, MAFDAL, became the heir to many of MAPAI's imperious policies as it grew together with the expansion of Israel into the West Bank and Gaza. MERETZ, on the other hand, promoted some of the more sensitive, conciliatory, and socialistic aspects of MAPAI when an earlier incarnation of it, RATZ (רצ), split from Labor in 1973. As one of the major partners in Rabin's peace coalition after the 1992 elections, MERETZ was instrumental in advancing the peace with the Palestinians.[63]

Hirsch's critique is only one example of the active part which Ha'ir took in the postzionist debates that raged in the country during the early 1990s. Shortly after the Oslo agreement was signed, the paper ran a series of articles examining some of the most hallowed axioms of Zionist history. "Are We a Western Democracy?" was one of them.[64] "Did the Jewish Religion Preserve the Jewish People?" was another, penned by Amnon Raz-Krakotzkin, an ardent postzionist.[65] Raz-Krakotzkin's claim was that Zionism has been an unfortunate mistake that only endangered Jews and did not protect them. His solution? Jews should return to the Diaspora, where their religion, not nationalism or military might, will preserve them as a people. Another accepted convention the paper examined read: "Is It Good to Die for Our Country?"[66] The title paraphrased the last words which one of the most famous Zionist pioneers, Yosef Trumpeldor, allegedly uttered on his deathbed after being fatally wounded in an Arab attack on a Jewish settlement in the Galilee in 1920. The piece ends with these words: "As long as the worship of the State and the willingness to die for it remain the central element [of Israeli culture], the future of death for the sake of the country is guaranteed."

As all of these articles attest, Ha'ir engaged with politics nontraditionally but directly, in addition to its less obvious work on behalf of a new civic and democratic Israel. For its first ten years the paper was a paragon of militant journalism that involved all levels of expression, thematic, stylistic, linguistic, economic, political, and visual. I want to conclude with two examples that illustrate the paper's own opinion about itself and about the significance of its contribution to the big changes that Israeli culture was undergoing then. The cover of the January 21, 1994, issue shows a map of the world with Shenkin Street drawn dispro-portionately big at its center. It is too easy to dismiss the cover as a smug expression of self-satisfaction. What is more telling, I think, is the funda-mental change of perspective that the map reveals. More than smarmy or indulgent, the picture is a symbol of the new focus or gravitational field of a post-national Israel. It is no longer the borders of the country that demarcate it and seclude it from other countries. All of these are fallen to the side, abandoned for the sake of a new civic agenda that em-phasizes culture, individuality, self-expression, and, yes, also good life.

Another example is a supplement that was added to the March 17, 1995, issue in which famous Israelis were photographed jumping in the air. The supplement was put together in the irreverent spirit of Purim and as homage to the famous American photographer, Philippe Hals-man, who took similar pictures of celebrities in 1955 (Audrey Hepburn, Marc Chagall, Brigitte Bardot). Although the photographic essay does not say it outright, the project itself and its publication close at the heel of Oslo discloses the euphoria that was felt by many Israelis at the time on the threshold of what seemed a new Middle Eastern era. Just as Halsman's pictures convey the widespread optimism that prevailed after World War II in the West, the Israeli variations on them exude hope and elation as well.

Like other contemporary media, *Ha'ir* and other week-lies expressed and shaped some of the most fundamental changes in the ways Israelis thought about themselves, about their country, and about their place in the region and the world. The new civic agenda the weekly promoted, and especially its celebration of consumerism, were eagerly seized by a public tired of an oppressive siege mentality and thirsty for better times, for a compensation for years of sacrifice and ab-stention. At the same time, the wholesale attack on the State and many of its venerable institutions and the aggressive promotion of individual self-expression had their limitations too. "The local weeklies during the 1980s," wrote Gal Uchovsky, "which fought against pomposity, accepted conventions . . . and especially against the conduct of the culture kings at the time, had one disadvantage: they did not believe in document-ing their dissatisfaction, preferring to insinuate it between the lines. In a country where Menahem Begin spoke in the name of 2000 years [of Jewish history] and six million [Holocaust victims], the local weeklies insisted on looking ahead one week at a time."[67]

While the change in focus was important and undermined some of the harmful jingoism that developed especially after the Six-Day War, the downside was a lack of a clear alternative agenda. The subversive promotion of existential detachment and non-commitment, the refusal to stand for anything and the insistence on communicating mainly through nonsense, eventually outlived their usefulness. This is essentially what Gadi Taub claims in his book about the dispirited rebellion. After the accord with the Palestinians was officially signed, the lack of direction was felt acutely because the dismissal of the old ways left a vacuum that was not filled by a clear future vision.

The romantic writers recorded and grappled in their works with many of the confusing sensibilities that Ha'ir articulated: the focus on consumerism, the loss of identity, and the loss of compassion in a post-national era. Unlike Ha'ir, however, their works did not just evince these changes but tried to examine their meaning as well. In a world that was rapidly disintegrating, where the traditional anchors of identity were being lifted without being replaced by others yet, the romantic writers tried to find new moorings. What they eventually settled on, even as an interim solution, was a new social arrangement that tried to overcome the alienation from the national group as well as the loneliness of individualism. What they suggested instead was an alternative option, that of romance.

Three

ETGAR KERET: A DISPIRITED REBEL WITH A CAUSE

Etgar Keret, who began writing as a young soldier in the early 1990s, was the most visible and prolific of the romantic writers. Keret sent his first stories to so-called lowbrow, popular media, such as the teenage weekly *Ma'ariv lano'ar* and the glossy women's magazines *At* and *La'isha*, because, as he confessed tellingly, it was more important for him to be read by the many than evaluated by the few.[1] Whether Keret meant this in earnest or not, popular and critical acclaim swiftly followed the publication of his first anthology of short stories, *Tsinorot* (*Pipelines*), in 1992. Both the reading public and the literary establishment doted on Keret almost from the start. His stories captivated disinterested teenagers as well as the hearts of more seasoned critics. Students in a problematic Bat-Yam high school, for instance, who usually had no stomach for literature, reacted enthusiastically after their teacher introduced them to some of Keret's stories: "See, that's the way to write! Short, with a little violence, a little sex and some humor besides. Now that's literature!"[2] Enthusiastic gut reactions of this kind were soon accompanied by more considered evaluations by leading writers and critics like Batya Gur, who pronounced Keret's stories "genuine works of art."[3]

Gur was not alone. The daily press throughout the 1990s was full of passionate critiques of Keret's stories which seem to have hit a public nerve. Common to most of these critiques is Keret's ability to succinctly express some of the seemingly irreconcilable tensions Al-Dror writes about; that is, the unbearable lightness of Israeli being in a post-national age. "A Wonderful Hell," reads Yehudit Orian's critique of *Pipelines* in the daily *Yediot Aharonot* (Feb. 28, 1992), which discusses the stories' preoccupation with "others" as a social category. So many of Keret's stories revolve around misfits, writes Orian, that the Other becomes the most well-defined group of the 1990s; a passive and haphazard collection of individuals that replaces the actively unified "we" of previous, more nationally minded generations. In another and more detailed critique of *Pipelines*, Fabiana Hefetz continues Orian's assessment by exploring the internal world of those misfits.[4] Keret's contemporary protagonists, writes Hefetz, live in a truly pluralistic universe; a morally defunct environment that has no clear or set system of values. However, through adroit literary manipulation readers find themselves enjoying what they would otherwise find offensive—bad language, violence, various descriptions of hell, and even death—almost as if they were watching a good TV show.

Hefetz recognizes Keret's existential angst but she also notes his particular writing style, his ability to translate the visual sensibility of a video clip into words, as a critical component of his popularity: the accessible, spoken idiom, the frenetic tempo, the accumulation of disparate cultural elements, the visual and verbal quotes, and the extreme brevity of the text. Keret's cinematic writing style has been noted by many, especially after the publication of his second anthology of short stories, *Ga'agu'ai Lekissinger* (*Missing Kissinger*), two years later in 1994. One critic who reviewed the new volume not only described Keret as a typical product of the mass media generation, but went even further to suggest that his allusions to popular TV series, comic books, and detective films is reminiscent of the way older Hebrew writers used biblical allusions.[5] This is a strong statement that puts Keret on a par with older masters of canonical literature and legitimizes his innovative incorporation of popular "low" culture by comparing it to the Bible.

That the writing style of young Keret appealed to his peers, to the first generation of Israelis who grew up with a substantial presence of commercial media, needs little explanation. His popularity in more judicious quarters is less obvious. One reason that may explain this agreement is the fairly quick way in which Keret came to be regarded as a postmodernist, a category that was bandied about freely in Israel in the early 1990s. Like any new critical method of inquiry, postmodernism drew a lot of attention as a novel method of cultural expression and analysis when it began to make inroads into the Israeli academy in the late 1980s and early 1990s.[6] Foucault's theory of power relations with its attendant relativism as a fundamental critical stance fit very well into the new historical and sociological accounts that gnawed at the foundations of old Zionism. Iconoclastic studies questioning the various truths of the Zionist story that began to emerge in the 1980s were boosted by the academic respectability of postmodernism, which doubts the legitimacy of any system of values, encompassing theories and grand narratives. Despite its instability as a systematic method of inquiry (as well as its own ironic adherence to an anti-narrative narrative), postmodernism thus became an especially powerful source for the winds of change that blew over Israel at that time.[7]

Because Keret's stories were written so "visually" and because many of them presented a confusing, mean, and hellish Israel, they were described fairly early on as quintessentially postmodern.[8] Even when critics did not literally define them as such, they pointed out many postmodern elements in Keret's works, like the influence of the mass media,[9] generic blurring,[10] the confusion of style and substance,[11] obscuring the boundaries between representation and reality,[12] and an ostensible disconnection between writer and narrator.[13] The influence of the mass media, especially films and television, is one of the most frequently mentioned postmodern features of Keret's writing. The stories are variably defined as good television shows (Hefetz), video clips (Gayer), and silhouettes in a silent film whose performative vocabulary is taken from movies, television, and print media (Gur). The lack of generic coordinates and the jumbled accumulation of disparate cultural artifacts are often perceived as the absence of a moral compass as well, a moral relativism that is revealed in the alleged absence of an implied narrator, the ephemeral principled voice usually invoked by the tension between the actual writer and the narrator he or she creates.[14]

Many of these signs can be detected even before reading Keret's actual stories by looking at the jackets of his anthologies. The 1992 *Pipelines*, for instance, features a detail from Edvard Munch's famous etching *The Scream*, which, significantly, is rendered in pink.[15] The choice of Munch's work highlights the haunting nature of many stories in the anthology, which remains Keret's most obviously political or socially aware work to date. The stories in *Pipelines* deal with the legacy of the Holocaust, Jewish-Arab relations, army service, the Intifada, and the dissolution of civil society in Israel because of the Palestinian uprising. At the same time, the very use of *The Scream*, which the cover serves up as a cliché of a cliché, in its choice of detail and the lurid pink instead of the dramatic darkness of the original painting, undermines the haunting dimension of the stories by manipulating the meaning of the etching through a manipulation of its surface, appearance, or "performance," to use postmodern parlance. The painful substance of the disturbing etching is not changed or removed but trifled with by cheerfully coloring it as if it were a drawing of a clown in a children's coloring book. The conversion of the original *Scream* into a pop-culture artifact relaxes the tension between the overwhelmingly articulate image and the raw and seemingly inarticulate etched lines that produce the work's effect in the first place. In other words, the pink color silences the scream by reversing what Andy Warhol did in his famous *Campbell's Soup* and other lithographs. Instead of elevating an ordinary, ubiquitous commercial product to the level of art in defiance of consumerism and mass production, which was what Warhol did, the jacket of *Pipelines* trivializes a unique and meaningful work of art and renders it insignificant, a squeak rather than a scream.[16]

A similar twist occurs in the jacket of Keret's second anthology, *Missing Kissinger*, which features a reproduction of *The Crying Child*, a sentimental painting that is probably the most recognizable icon of kitsch in Israel, sold in popular street markets as posters, oil paintings, painted rugs, etc. The kitschy quality of the picture resides in the utter lack of ambivalence about the rosy-faced little boy with his sandy hair, sad, blue eyes, button nose, and sweet, red lips. Even the tears that trickle down the boy's plump cheeks are meant to highlight the simple emotional effect of the image at the expense of a more complex artistic engagement. One of the outstanding aspects of the garish portrait, and indeed of kitsch in general, is its excess, the overabundance of sentimentalism, sensationalism, melodrama, and romance that finally numbs viewers to any and all of these emotions.[17] Many stories in the anthology are presented through similar excess; through the accumulation of familiar cultural references and quotes that ostensibly stay at surface level and never leave it to reflect on it by providing a more distant perspective.

One of the most obvious examples of this is the second story in *Kissinger*, "So Good" (*Kol kach tov*). The story follows Itsik, who is determined to keep Happiness, Opportunity, Pure Pleasure, and Success from entering his home and enticing him. After fortifying his cabin by lining the chimney with sharp knives and by electrifying the door handles, Itsik sits on his bed in his pajamas and cowboy boots and waits for the onslaught, shotgun in hand. But although he puts up a good fight, blasting Opportunity, shooting his TV set to keep the Family Channel away, impaling Success while trying to think about terrible things like starving Africans, the Holocaust, breast cancer victims, and the homeless, he finally realizes that he is fighting a losing battle:

> He didn't have a chance. The smile grew wider and wider, threatening to swallow him. Three emotions he didn't recognize already surrounded him, taking his gear off, wiping the number off his arm with a little spit, changing his

"Why?" T-shirt with another one that read "Don't Worry Be Happy." Don't worry, it's going to be OK, he tried to cheer himself up as he was dragged out. She'll be there, waiting for you, you'll have a good time. You'll have a car. The anticipation turned his knees to jelly. You'll have it so good, damn it, so good.

The tears in his throat dried completely. Outside, the trees were green. The Sky too. It wasn't too hot or too cold. A van covered with drawings of the Simpsons and with ads for mortgage was already waiting for him downstairs. [My translation]

On its surface, the story seems like a textbook example of postmodernist writing. It reads like an easily recognized script for an action film or television series, full of references to pop culture, including the names of television channels (HBO), television shows (*The Cosby Show, The Simpsons*), and television characters (Lisa Bonet's, from *The Cosby Show*), and various consumer goods and services (Club Med, take-away pizza). Moreover, the pop-cultural universe that is invoked by these references is made even more vivid by occasional one-liners from real or imagined action films, like "she is expendable," transliterated in Hebrew letters, or "think about something nice, bitch, on your way to heaven," etc.

Just like the picture on the anthology's jacket, the shallowness of the virtual world that the story sets up is produced by its excess; by the story's tendency to over-communicate. The story is packed with artifacts, gestures, and modes of speech that repeatedly and blatantly identify it as a generic video space devoid of any national-specific characteristics, including cowboy boots, shotguns, zombies, soap operas, a fireplace, cable TV, techno music, and the cabin in which the action takes place. Most of these are not readily identifiable as part of Israeli reality or culture. They are quotes from an imagined video universe. Even the specificity that the Hebrew of the story would presumably give it is neutralized and made generic by the heavily anglicized syntax and lexicon. In addition to obvious non-Hebrew words and phrases, like "take-away" and "full volume," which are actually transliterated, most of the story is written in a jarring English syntax. Sentences like "I hate my pizzas cold" (קרות אני שונא את הפיצות שלי), or "it must be the roof" (זה חייב להיות הגג) clearly originated in English and sound awkward in Hebrew.[18]

The same may be said about another of the presumably authentic Israeli referents in the story, the occasional use of military parlance to describe the action that packs the narrative. Modes of speech that originate in the Israeli army have long been influencing contemporary Israeli Hebrew. But when the militarization of Israeli society is broadened and injected even into the virtual world of mass entertainment, both realms change in the process. The Israeli Defense Forces acquire the quality of a show, an amusing diversion, while the diverting story gains the intensity and consequence of military action; a process that flattens or empties both. "They always send it first," the narrator reports about the approaching Success, "like some kind of a Bedouin tracker," referring to a common IDF practice to attach Bedouin soldiers as trackers to field combat units. At the same time, Pure Pleasures sneaks up to the house with take-away pizzas and pornographic magazines in order to provide "cover" for it (רִחֵק); that is, engage the enemy with fire from one direction while another unit approaches it from a different side.

Stylistically, then, the story abounds with loud, disparate elements that draw a lot of attention to form at the expense of content. However, the story clearly has a message as well, an almost didactic moralism that censures commercialism and consumerism, the false opportunities they provide, and their bogus promise of happiness. The protagonist is driven to such rage and violence because twice in his life he was betrayed by people he loved who tried to numb his sense of disappointment and loss with artificial substitutes, like sappy television shows and romantic vacations. "This time he'll be ready," he vows to himself as he sits on his bed, waiting for the invasion of his body's snatchers. "It won't be like back then, at his parents' home. They won't make a smiling zombie out of him, someone who loves soap operas . . . and kisses his mother whenever possible." Although this is not entirely clear, it seems that the protagonist was traumatized as a young child by the separation of his parents, who then compensated for the pain it caused their child by letting him watch TV freely and pretended everything was fine. His second trauma involves the painful separation from the girlfriend he loved. "He is going to teach them a thing or two about happiness," he thinks resolutely after booby-trapping the chimney. "Five years at Club Med. Five fucking years. With a girl he loved, oral and anal sex, money like garbage. He took it the hardest way possible."

The protagonist's violent rage is not directed at Happiness itself. In fact, he remains an optimist and a romantic at heart to the very end. Even after he is overpowered by the forces that invade his house and drag him out he tries to cheer himself up by imagining how his beloved will be waiting for him there. His knees buckle and feel like jelly when he imagines the good times they may still have together. His problem is not the belief in happiness but its false representations, the many obstacles that modern culture puts in the way of achieving it in the form of alluring but bogus substitutes.

Many of Keret's allegedly postmodern stories promote such surprisingly naïve, old-fashioned, and even conservative ideals like patriotism, heroism, true friendship, and especially true love, or at least the pursuit of it. This has not been the most common reading of them, although it was among the first. In one of the earliest interviews with the young writer, Gil Hovav declared Keret the first Jewish musketeer: "Finally, we too have a charming and adventurous gunslinger, quick tempered and ready to fight, someone who will do everything he can to save his lady or civilization." Considering the clear system of values in Keret's 1992 *Pipelines*, writes Hovav, values that include honor, honesty, manliness, loyalty, and a sense of adventure, one wonders if this interdisciplinary musketeer was born in the right century.[19]

Even those stories that initially shocked and confused readers and earned Keret a defiant, rebellious reputation actually promote a bourgeois, civilized world above all, a bourgeois civilization that may be completely warped, but whose mangled remains desperately grasp at lost ideals of propriety, respect, fairness, chivalry, and especially romance.[20] Although much of Keret's language and plots make this assessment sound initially strange, two of the shortest stories in *Pipelines* illustrate this point convincingly. The first story is called "Hubeza."[21] Since the story is very short, I translate here in full:

> There is this place called Hubeza, not far from Tel-Aviv. I was told that people in Hubeza wear black all the time and that they are always happy. "I don't believe this nonsense," said my best friend, who really meant to say he doesn't believe that there are happy people. Many people don't believe. So I boarded the bus that goes to Hubeza and all the way there I listened to war songs on my Walkman. The people in Hubeza never die in wars. People in Hubeza don't go to the army. I got off the bus in the central square. The people of Hubeza welcomed me very warmly. From close up it was very easy to see how happy they really were. They dance a lot in Hubeza and read thick books, and I danced next to them in Hubeza and read their thick books. And I wore their clothes in Hubeza and slept in their beds.

And I ate their food in Hubeza and kissed their babies, on the mouth. For three whole weeks. But happiness is not contagious.

Although the narrator is searching for happiness, his search involves only the pursuit of its exterior signs, like dancing. His obsession with the performative or superficial qualities of happiness, which cannot really be taken for a verifiable indication of a genuine emotion, replaces what we would expect to be a much longer and more rigorous inner journey. The narrator's casual search for one of life's oldest and most fundamental quests, his short bus ride to a nearby destination, and his leisurely stay there as if he were a vacationing tourist, ironically validates and magnifies the pathos of the desire for happiness. At the same time, the brevity of the text and the expectation of a quick fix that would be achieved by a change of scenery, clothing, or reading material identify the text as a product of a capitalist, consumerist culture that relentlessly promotes the belief that such fundamental changes can indeed take place through the purchase or procurement of certain manufactured goods.[22]

The other story, "Shlomo, Homo, You Mother-Fucking Fag" (*Shlomo, homo, kus el omo*) reads almost like a prolonged joke that deals much more crudely and harshly with a similar theme. Shlomo is a miserable schoolboy who is picked on by his classmates during a class trip to the park. The teacher, who ostensibly is the only one who feels compassion for him, tries to comfort him some during the trip. But when at the end of the day Shlomo asks her pathetically: "Miss, why do all the kids hate me?" the teacher shrugs her tired shoulders, puffs on her cigarette, and replies casually: "How should I know, I'm only the substitute teacher." While the story deals flippantly with a harsh injustice, it offers no explanation or consolation for it. In many ways it even exacerbates the injustice and the atmosphere of violence and aggression by adding the epithets from the title to Shlomo's name every time it is mentioned. The teacher, who significantly is a substitute teacher, not a "real" one, like the park, the artificial lake, and the giant statue of an orange, which are all mockups of Zionist achievements, goes through the motions and helps Shlomo only because it is part of her job description. That she has no real compassion for the child becomes clear in the end, when she cannot or will not offer the boy any words of consolation. The boy is thus left alone in the desert of a new Israeli society that does not make a real effort to provide a meaningful message that would unite its disparate elements under a redeeming narrative.

Gil Hovav was not the only reader who identified the wistfully idyllic qualities of Keret's stories, in which love played a central role, although he was one of the only critics who stated it so clearly. Several other readers recognized the strong element of protest in the stories, which disapprove of the hellish reality they portray, and hide their loud lament behind the busy, over-crowded surface.[23] Many of Keret's stories offer much more specific critiques of Israeli society and culture than the more generalized laments raised by the two stories above. Stories like "Siren" (Tsfira), "Nylon," "The Son of the Head of the Mossad" (Haben shel rosh hamosad), "An Arab with a Moustache" (Aravi im safam), "Arkadi Hilwe Takes the Number Five" (Arkadi Hilwe nose'ah bekav chamesh), and "Cocked and Locked" (Daruch venatsur), to name a few, deal directly with some of the most troubling aspects of Israeli society, like the legacy of the Holocaust, the militarization of Israeli society, its treatment of Arabs, and the moral consequences of its prolonged control of the Palestinian territories.

"Siren," for instance, while ostensibly dealing with the legacy of the Holocaust, is a harsh comment on the country's fallen ideals or their corruption. The story takes place in a high school around Independence Day, which in Israel is preceded by Holocaust Remembrance Day and Fallen Soldiers' Remembrance Day. It involves a conflict between an awkward but principled hero and two school bullies, Gilad and Sharon; two star students and athletes who plan to serve in elite army units. In fact, Sharon cannot take part in the Holocaust commemoration ceremony in school because he is away undergoing the last entry examination to the marine commandos. When he comes back, he celebrates his acceptance into the commandos by vandalizing the bicycle of the school's janitor, an old Holocaust survivor. After the protagonist reports the vandalism to the school's principal, Sharon and Gilad plan to punish him for snitching on them. But just as the bullies are about to lay their hands on him the wail of the sirens commemorating Israel's fallen soldiers begins to rise, stopping them in their tracks.

> I looked at them standing like two mannequins and all my fear was suddenly gone. Gilad, who stood erect with his eyes shut holding Sharon's jacket in his hand, looked like a big coat hanger. And Sharon, with the murderous look on his face and his clenched fist suddenly looked like a little boy who is trying to mimic a move he once saw in an action movie. I passed through the hole in the fence and went away slowly and quietly. Behind me, I heard Sharon mutter,

"You'll see, we'll kick the shit out of you," but he didn't move an inch. I continued walking home, passing by people who stood frozen like wax figures, the siren enveloping me like an invisible shield.

The story juxtaposes Israel's military legacy with the country's legacy of the Holocaust. Ostensibly Sharon and Gilad are the apple of the eye of a Zionist establishment who set out to make warriors out of weak Jews like Scholem, the school's Holocaust-surviving janitor, precisely in order to prevent such disasters. But the Golem, as the Hebrew saying goes, has risen against its creator. The two bullies are devoid of any sense of the moral responsibility that should accompany power and be part of army service, especially in Israel. In fact, like many young Israelis today who volunteer to serve in elite units, they view army service as a form of extreme sport, to be endured as a personal rather than a more national or civic challenge. This is why Gilad flirts with the pretty Sivan during the Holocaust commemoration service, and it is also why Sharon does not even attend, preferring to undergo a military checkup instead. That the army even scheduled the examination on Holocaust Remembrance Day indicts the society at large, not just the two high school kids.

On a more literal level, the connections between the IDF and the Holocaust are maintained also in the fact that Scholem, the janitor, was in the Sonderkommando, the group of inmates who were charged with removing dead bodies from the gas chambers at Auschwitz. The ignorant young protagonist cannot imagine "our small and skinny Scholem in any kind of commando unit," certainly not compared with the smart, handsome, and athletic Sharon. But the juxtaposition between the just and diminutive diasporic Jew and the unjust athletic Israeli serves as a rebuke to a society which is either so amnesic or so corrupt that it forgot or ignores some of the fundamental historical justifications for its existence as well as some of the ideological tenets that it strove for.[24] The protagonist ostensibly flaunts the reverential ritual to stand still while the siren sounds, but his higher sense of morality is rewarded by the protection it gives him. Almost magically, the siren seems to freeze everyone, including the two bullies who are exposed as phonies when they mutter violent threats against the protagonist while pretending to respect the memory of the dead.

The army and by extension Israel's other security agencies like the Mossad are frequently exposed in Keret's stories as abusive organizations, who have long lost sight of their original purpose or have outlived their usefulness. Populated by men like Gilad and Sharon, they misuse their power by terrorizing supposed enemies of the State, most often Arabs, as well as their own members and members of their society. The army looms large in Keret's stories no doubt because it was one of his most profound, recent experiences as a young Israeli man. But the resonance of the theme in the culture at large, especially with younger people, who were Keret's most eager readers, also attests to the importance of the IDF as an acculturating agency. The army is one of the first meaningful introductions Israelis get to their society as young, independent adults, and its influence on them is deep and enduring. The abuse many of Keret's protagonists encounter in the army is therefore indicative of society's general state of degeneracy and functions as an expression and a symbol of it.

The cruelty, violence, and vulgarity of Israeli society are so oppressive in the story "Nylon" that it drives Alon Hasin, the new army recruit at the center of it, to suicide. As long as he is passively abused by the system, the young soldier is willing to endure it somehow, but once he discovers that his own humanity is also compromised by it he opts out. "You call this nylon, Hasin?" the sergeant yells at the new recruit, whose name ironically means "durable oak" in Hebrew. "This sheet of plastic has a hole in it the size of a cunt." Putting his face close to Alon's the sergeant then whispers loudly, "Did you ever see a cunt, Hasin?" and when Alon faintly replies in the negative, the sergeant tells him to "go ask your mother nicely, maybe she'll show you where [a dud like you] came from." Alon is so eager to improve his soldierly performance that after trying hard to wrap all his gear tightly in nylon as he was ordered he continues to wrap himself in nylon too. From now on neither the spit of the yelling sergeant nor the dirt he crawls in as punishment for various lapses sticks to him. But when he finds out that the nylon also isolates him from his own emotions and from the rest of the world, making him apathetic and cold, Alon decides to quit. "He looked at himself in the mirror, at the shiny unit tag, at the starched uniform, at the razor in his right hand. He drew the razor close to the artery in his throat. 'Basic training is over,' he whispered, 'the nylon can be cut open.'" In a manner typical of many of Keret's heroes, the young man prefers to direct his aggression inward rather than engage with the outside world about it. Given Alon's status as a quintessential member of the dispirited rebellion, his protest is meek too, literally confined to his own body.

In other stories the aggression is less contained, as in "The Son of the Head of the Mossad," a chilling tale about generational miscommunication, neglect, moral irresponsibility, and criminal apathy. "The son of the head of the Mossad didn't even know that he was the son of the head of the Mossad," begins the story. "He thought his dad was a heavy equipment contractor. And when every morning his dad would take his Beretta out of the bottom drawer and examine the special 0.38 bullets in his magazine one by one he thought it was because his father worked with Arabs from the territories." Although the father engages in the brutal work of literally eliminating Israel's enemies, his son is seemingly unaware of his gruesome employment. But his ignorance is suspect not only because the explanation he supplies for it—that his father works with Palestinians—is problematic. The son's ignorance is compounded by the apathy that makes him an accessory to his father's brutality. "On the days [the head of the Mossad] came home late he would smile a tired smile at the son of the head of the Mossad and at his mother and say, 'Don't ask what a day I had.' And they didn't and went back to watching TV or doing homework. He wouldn't have told them anyway, even if they did ask." Both the mother and the son probably know or at least suspect what the father does. After all, he is freely wielding a gun around the house. But by keeping silent about it they condone it in effect.

The story uses the domestic habits of a secret agent symbolically. The story's very name as well as its other formulaic aspects point at it. The cryptic reference to the father's identity, repeated over and over again, is a parody of the exaggerated veneration Israelis have for the Mossad and its leaders; a veneration that extends to many of the country's security agencies and that, according to this interpretation of the story, has reached unhealthy proportions.[25] The enigmatic reference to the son's identity makes the parody all too clear, since there is no need to protect it even if the son's father heads the Mossad.

But the real problem in the story arises when the tacit approval of the father's actions inspires the son to follow in his footsteps, albeit with none of the father's justifications. The moral ambiguity of the service that the Mossad's head provides his country is somewhat redeemed by the hard work he puts in day in and day out and by the emotional toll it takes on him. His job as the State's executioner evidently made him a bitter, silent man and contributed to his dysfunction as a family man. The same cannot be said about the son, however, who succumbs to the corrupting influence of his father's profession when he takes out the gun one day and kills a kid who humiliated him in school. "At two o'clock the son of the head of the Mossad finished his lunch and said he was going out to play basketball. In the evening, when the son of the head of the Mossad returned home he smiled a tired smile at his father and mother and said, 'Don't ask what a day I had,' and they didn't. Afterwards, when his father went to the bathroom and his mother was asleep already, he returned the gun to the bottom drawer. He wouldn't have told them anyway, even if they did ask."

The son is deliberately characterized as a sensitive weakling in contrast to his "cowboy" father in order to highlight the change or transition he undergoes. The father belonged to an older generation, whose commitment and determination was shaped by the country's more dire beginnings. In part, this is the justification for his role in the Mossad. But since the son grew up in a different and more secure Israel, he has no use for his father's grim resolve. Herein lies the essence of the generational gap that separates father and son. Instead of grooming himself to stand guard on his country's borders, like his father, the son spends time with his girlfriend in his room, talking with her tenderly for hours. The father sees such normal teenage behavior as wimpy and unmanly. He would have preferred instead that his son be more like his friend Lihu, who is tall and strong and silent and who "in some respects was much better suited to be the son of the head of the Mossad than the real son." As a result of the clash between his father's misplaced expectations and his inability to live up to them the son snaps. In an effort to please his father the son takes up his gun and uses it to kill someone. The difference is symbolic, of course. The father kills to protect the community and is therefore sanctioned by it, while the son kills for personal reasons. One is a soldier, the other a murderer. The legacy that the father bequeaths his son is devastating because even if he does kill in self-defense, his violent way of life becomes an example for his son. But since the son is physically and mentally unfit to carry on with his father's work, his attempt to do so results in a monstrous twisting of that legacy.

Keret's descriptions of a distorted Israeli soul continue in the story "An Arab with a Moustache," in which the Jewish perception of Arabs and the relations with them reach psychotic proportions. The story combines appalling racism and xenophobia with existential Jewish fears in a horrifying concoction that has been seeping ever deeper into Israeli identity and politics since 1967.[26] "An Arab with a moustache boarded the bus," begins the story, which promises to continue predictably enough for anyone who has followed the news about suicide bombers on Israeli buses since the first Intifada. But the story takes a different direction. The Arab, readers find out, is an innocent passenger, though this does not interfere with the narrator's hysterical conviction that he is a terrorist who will draw out a knife and stab him the minute he turns his back to him. Ironically, both the Arab and the Jew fear each other. After accidentally stepping on the narrator's foot the Arab says "excuse me, excuse me, excuse me, his mustache prickling my hand. These Arabs have mustaches like wires. From fear I said to him, 'yalla, beat it, you stinker.'" Neither can put aside his fears of the other.

Most alarming, though, is the crude and hateful reaction that the fear of the Arab strikes in the Jewish narrator. Tormented by visions of carnage that have become part of everyday life in Israel since the first Intifada, the narrator quite literally goes mad in the bus. The illogic of the first two sentences makes this apparent. It is never clear who exactly boards the bus because the announcement declaring "an Arab with a mustache boarded the bus" that opens the story is immediately followed by "even if there was nothing Arabic about him, even if he were not an Arab at all, you'd be able to see that he was Arab by his mustache." The narrator's psychosis is so deep that it defies reality, all the more so when that reality includes a bloody history that encumbers understanding and compromises it in the first place.

Fomented by his fear and hatred the narrator becomes hysterical, making up in his head delirious justifications for his suspicions, which he then tries to share with others on the bus, confusing imagination with reality. "They always sit in the back," the narrator begins a frothing train of thought about the alleged Arab, "so that you'd have to wonder if they are going to sneak up on you with a knife or not, and turn back all the time and strain your neck. And then they never do, the innocent lambs, and who ends up with a stiff neck? People like you and me while they come out clean." The speech makes no sense but it confirms the obsession of the narrator, who has apparently lost his mind from fear. "And it's all because we are not tough enough with them," he then turns to a fellow passenger, continuing a conversation he began in his head. "It was important for me to make friends with him," he explains, "so he'd warn me if the Arab behind me draws a knife from his basket." Blinded by his fears, the narrator hallucinates about a world full of imaginary enemies and lashes out at them. In the context of Israel's bloody history of suicide bombings the narrator's initial fear of the mustachioed passenger is certainly understandable. But just as in the previous story, prolonged exposure to such conditions—that is, Israel's deadly conflict with its Arab neighbors—can have very negative consequences. The author does not just indict the story's protagonist for his racial fanaticism but warns about the causes that bring it about as well.

Keret's deep social involvement is conspicuous even in an aggressively postmodern story like "Arkadi Hilwe Takes the Number Five." The title of the story offers the first hint about the tight symbiosis in the story between style and content as well as the volatile potential of its disparate elements; a potential that is fully realized in the story. Although the title reads like a smooth colloquialism, a casual reference to someone's bus ride, the discord begins with the passenger's name. Arkadi is an obvious Russian name. Hilwe is an obvious Arabic name. Joining them together as someone's first and last name is immediately jarring to Israeli ears. The number five bus is also significant, not just because it traverses Dizzengoff Street, Tel-Aviv's central and most symbolic street that often stands for the city itself. One of the first and most devastating suicide bombing attacks in Israel would take place aboard that bus in October of 1994, marking a shift in the war with the Palestinians that eventually led to the withdrawal from Gaza and parts of the West Bank more than ten years later.

True to its title, the story continues to describe an especially horrific Israel, a terrifying universe devoid of compassion, a disintegrating society awash with blood whose conflicting elements clash violently with one another in a cacophonous fight. The story is packed to excess with gruesome images that are delivered with a chilling detachment that accentuates the horror. The first words that open the story are "son of a bitch," uttered by a fat drunkard who is waiting at the bus station with Arkadi, spoiling for a fight. Arkadi ignores him and continues to read his paper, which is plastered with gory pictures of mutilated bodies. "I am talking to you," the drunkard persists, adding the epithet "stinking Arab" for good measure. "Russian, Arkadi replied, hastening to hide behind the side of his family that was not maligned yet. My mother is from Riga. Sure, said the fat man with disbelief, and your father? From Nablus, admitted Arkadi and returned to his paper to look at a picture of Burnt Kurdish dwarfs flung out of a giant toaster and another picture of a lynching."

The vulgar belligerence of the drunkard and the grisly pictures in the paper are but a prelude to a story that reveals a *Clockwork Orange*–like world of senseless, random violence that is fueled by the disparate ethnic and political factions that make up Israeli society, culture, and history. Arkadi responds with chilling violence to the drunk's persistent nagging. "It was five o'clock and the bus did not arrive yet. In a speech on the radio the Prime Minister promised rivers of blood and the fat man was a head taller than him. [Arkadi] kicked the fat man's balls with his knee and followed it immediately with the crowbar he hid between the pages of the paper. The fat man fell to the ground and began crying, Arabs! Russians! Help! Arkadi gave him another smack on the head with the crowbar and sat back on the bench."

The frightening miscommunication continues in Arkadi's conversation with the bus driver, with an old passenger, and finally with his mother. Don't worry about him, "he's epileptic," Arkadi tells the bus driver, who wants to help the sprawled and spasmodic fat man. "If he's epileptic, where is all the blood from," the driver inquires. "From the Prime Minister's speech on the radio," Arkadi replies apathetically. Once inside the bus, Arkadi offers an old passenger to help him solve his crossword puzzle. "Was I talking to you, you stinking Arab," the old man snaps at Arkadi. In a twist on a crossword-puzzle definition, Arkadi rejoins with "a question often used by Border Patrol policemen (28 letters)." Minutes later he gets off the bus and as it drives off he ducks behind a garbage bin, anticipating the blast of the explosives he just left on it. "The explosion came seconds later, covering Arkadi with trash." Coming home he finds his grandmother sitting in a tent on their roof deck watching a commercial on TV in which a sexy swimsuit model "was swimming the backstroke in a river of blood that flowed along Arlozorov Street." Arkadi fantasizes about having sex with the model and does not hear his mother, who is trying to tell him that his grandfather was crucified this morning at the central bus station during a special operation to enforce parking regulations. "Are you talking to me?" he asks her. "No, I am talking to God," his mother replies angrily and curses in Russian. "Oh, Arkadi said in return and went back to the TV. The picture now focused on the model's lower body parts. The slimy blood flowed all around them without touching them. There was a supertitle above it and the emblem of the city, but Arkadi resisted the temptation to read it."

It is not hard to follow the different elements of Israeliana that crowd this short story: recent Russian immigrants, dissipate Israeli youth—fat, lazy, and gone bad—Arabs, the Arab-Israeli conflict, the Intifada, the greater conflict in the Middle East, suicide bombings, social disparity, injustice, violence, racism, political cynicism, and above all the apathy of a society that has been flooded ad nauseam with all of these images by an invidious mass media that replicates and amplifies them until they cease to make sense. The end of the story exemplifies the gory, macabre collage that makes it and by extension the Israel that it describes. Each of its pieces is packed with so much symbolism that it quite literally explodes or collapses and loses its ability to represent anything in a meaningful way.

Among the elements in this story that make no sense, the protagonist, Arkadi, is the least possible, a textual contrivance that highlights the text's postmodern stance. Although all literary characters are essentially textual inventions, they are inventions based on key mimetic values such as individualization, psychology, complexity, and depth.[27] In modernist texts characters are ontologically secure beings that construct the text and produce its meaning. Readers decipher the literary conventions and codes that make up a character and assemble them by translating these conventions into a coherent image drawn from recognized life experiences. In postmodernism, however, the process of assemblage is tampered with so that characters fail to develop a personality and become instead textual effects, empty signifiers that point nowhere. In extreme cases—Arkadi, for instance—the postmodern character is not representative at all but illustrative, a cartoon that cannot be read for psychological subtext or representation of identity but as a political and social illustration of an ideological reality.

As a Russian Arab Arkadi is a conceivable character, but not a very plausible one. He is a signifier that cannot be easily signified in contemporary Israel, where Jews and Arabs rarely socialize and seldom marry. But even if he were, his political allegiance makes his character more improbable still. As an Arab-Jew blowing up Israeli Jews, Arkadi is cutting his nose off to spite his face. His very being negates itself so that he no longer refers to a recognized reality and exists only as a self-referential linguistic entity. By drawing attention to the impossibility of representation, the notion of a literary character itself is deconstructed here. Arkadi thus becomes a stylistic device, a "wordy" creation that eliminates the mimesis of reality in fiction and causes the character to collapse into the discourse, as Buchweitz writes.[28]

Arkadi cannot be subjected to traditional categories of interpretation because those fail to explain him adequately. It is at this juncture that Keret's style becomes his message, like that of Castel-Bloom. The writer's inability to cope with an uncertain, unstable, and insecure Israeli reality is conveyed through the abuse of literary norms designed to lament the loss of direction, meaning, and ideals. The textual chaos simulates disillusionment. Instead of attempting to pursue authenticity, the text abandons it and promotes the corruption of narrative conventions as a comment on a world that exhibits a similar disruption or collapse.

One of the most effective ways in which narrative technique is corrupted in the story is the maintenance of a superficial, textual level that connects the story's disparate elements seamlessly. The story is made up of a string of jarring scenes or situations that are linked only because they are placed next to one another on a continuum. But almost none of them flows from what precedes it in the way we usually expect a traditional narrative to progress.

"Son of a bitch," the fat man muttered and hit his fist hard
against the bench of the bus station where he was sitting.
Arkadi continued to look at the pictures in the paper,
ignoring completely the words around them. Time went by
slowly. Arkadi hated waiting for buses. "Son of a bitch," said
the fat man again, this time more loudly and spat on the
pavement close to Arkadi's feet. "Are you talking to me?"
Arkadi asked, somewhat surprised and raised his eyes from
the paper to meet the alcohol-shot eyes of the fat man. "No,
I'm talking to my ass," the fat man yelled. "Oh," said Arkadi
and returned to his paper. The paper had a color picture of
mutilated bodies heaped high in the city square.

Although the fat man announces himself loudly and crudely, Arkadi
is oblivious to his existence. Not because he is uncomfortable or afraid
of him, as we later learn, and as most people would be in a similar situation. Arkadi simply does not see him or hear him and engages in a
leisurely reading of his paper, dwelling on the mundane inconvenience
of waiting for public transportation. Nothing in his behavior belies the
ominous fact that he is a violent terrorist who will execute his mission
in cold blood in a few moments. The mission itself is unimagined because Arkadi is presumed Jewish. Like the bloody pictures in the paper
that are separated from their explanatory text, Arkadi remains cryptic as
well, undecipherable. His literal reaction to the fat man's facetious reply,
"No, I'm talking to my ass," only simulates understanding, underscoring
the lack of communication between them or even the willingness to do
so. So is Arkadi's final refusal or inability to read the supertitle on TV,
which functions as a symbolic writing on the wall. Arkadi is a symbol in
a world populated by symbols. Without an intermediary he cannot inter-
pret or comprehend his surroundings.

Perhaps this is why some critics believed Keret's works bespoke despair and evinced a sense of gloom and helplessness about the state of
the country. Author Yoram Kaniuk, who himself took part in the cultural
revolution that transformed Israel after 1948 from a centralized pioneering society to a more pluralistic and liberal one, commented with a mixture of admiration and regret on Keret's generation. Kaniuk delighted in
the lean language of the young writers, in which he may have found an
expression of his own efforts at limbering the stiffer pioneering Hebrew
of his day.[29] But he saw little connection between their mode of writing
and the cultural agenda he and his peers promoted in the first decades

after statehood. Young writers, comedians, and journalists today, Kaniuk wrote, seem to have abandoned the greater idea of the State in favor of a new kingdom, that of the city of Tel-Aviv, which they made into the capital of its own culture. This kingdom, he contends, has nothing to do with age-old Jewish traditions (נצח ירושלים) or with the more recent Zionist heritage (יפי הלילות בכנען). Keret's generation, Kaniuk seems to be saying, is not interested in carrying on a dialogue with former literary traditions, as his and former literary generations did, for instance. This is a generation content to shut itself in a Tel-Aviv of its imagination, detached from the rest of the country, floating in a vacuum.

Urbanity as a sign of sophistication, complexity, and artifice as well as a designation of place was indeed one of the most distinct features of the romantic writers. Generally, it was understood as a defiant stance against what Kaniuk calls Zionist heritage, much of which valorized the land and vilified the city for reasons that had to do with Zionism's own revolutionary agenda. Perhaps this is why some readers understood Keret's hyper-urban spaces as an expression of despair; despair of contemporary Israeli reality, as Gavriel Moked also writes.[30] A society that is hermetically confined to the kind of urban spaces it occupies in the romantic literature must be ailing, these critics mused, especially if one measures it against Zionist ideals that sought to sever the connection between Jews and the city. That this should be so even if most of the ethics that animated early Zionism faded by the time of this critique is owed to the mythological hold Zionist ideals had on a culture that was created in their image. So much so, in fact, that Moked wondered whether the sense of hopelessness he perceived in Keret was also the origin and reason for what he saw as the simplistic form of his works, their flatness, their two-dimensionality, their comic-strip quality.[31] In other words, Moked wonders whether the ideological degeneration of Zionism is reflected in the formal defects of Keret's writing.

The confusion which Kaniuk and Moked felt about Keret and his peers is strange because both critics identify some of the core issues that constitute the literary dialogue that Keret continued with his literary predecessors without identifying it as such. But as "Arkadi" and many of Keret's other stories make clear, the sense of despair clearly denotes a confusion and exasperation with a society that had lost its vision and meaningful frame of ideological reference. Stylistically, Keret's stories create what Jameson has called "the waning of affect," that is, the peculiar postmodern dynamic whereby the subject is fragmented and liberated not just from anxiety but "from every other kind of feeling as well."[32]

But this postmodern patina is misleading, and should certainly not be read as literary negligence or incompetence. Keret's Israel is populated by apathetic, black-and-white stick figures as a stance against a treacherous reality that has flattened rounder figures and made their existence doubtful and problematic. His engagement with the times differs from the temporal engagement of his literary forerunners only in kind but not in principle. His alleged withdrawal from contemporary Israeli life—Kaniuk and Moked probably mean the traditional commitment of Israeli authors to social issues—ensconcing himself in a semi-virtual urban bubble called Tel-Aviv, marks the peculiar passive aggression that distinguishes his generation. Unable or unwilling to influence a dysfunctional, morally relative culture that seems to lack the instinct for social and cultural reform, Keret and other contemporary writers retreat to more confined worlds of their own making over which they have much better control: they can warp them in a frustrated act of displacement or attempt to re-create them on a smaller and more manageable scale.

This is where the preoccupation with love and the precedence it receives over much else comes into play: the longing for a romantic refuge or cocoon that would let them escape from or at the very least shrink the mean world around them to a smaller, more manageable scale. Although Keret's dejected heroes often fail to find love, and punish themselves by directing their aggression against their own person, they still seek meaning and solace in the pursuit of love. These opposite solipsistic expressions—passive aggression and emotional fulfillment—that transpire within the confines of one's own privately created world, mark an easing of the tension between individual and community that was the hallmark of modern Hebrew literature since its beginning. Most of the works of other romantic writers share this sensibility as well, in which the desire and search for True Love becomes an organizing principle of redemptive significance.

A simple statistical examination of Keret's work so far will clearly show how in the four collections of short stories he published between 1992 and 2002—*Pipelines*, 1992, *Missing Kissinger*, 1994, *Kneller's Happy Campers* (*Hakaytana shell kneller*), 1998, and *Cheap Moon* (*Anihu*), 2002—the number of stories devoted to relationships, not just with women actually, but with male friends and even with pets, but always and repeatedly relationships involving two, has increased from a fifth of the stories in the first anthology, *Pipelines*, to two-thirds of the stories in the last anthology, *Cheap Moon*. And this peculiar fact holds true for Keret's contemporaries as well, Taub, Weil, and Amir, who published less than Keret during that same time, but whose collections of short stories—always short stories—deal primarily with the dynamics of romance in urban settings.

Love, romance, or abiding friendships gradually emerge in Keret's works as answers to some of the existential confusion they portray, to a world that lost its moral compass and makes little sense. This happens already in the last story in Keret's first anthology, *Pipelines*, a story called "Crazy Glue" (*Devek meshuga*), in which a married couple is isolated from everyone and everything around them in a brief moment of connubial bliss. In the story, the couple's relationship is threatened by an affair the husband has with a colleague at work. Fearful that his wife suspects the affair, the husband decides to come home early one day instead of staying out late with his mistress. On his return he discovers that his wife glued down everything in the house: "I tried to move one of the chairs and sit on it. It didn't move. I tried again. Not even a millimeter. She glued it to the floor. The refrigerator didn't open either, she glued it too." The narrator finally finds his wife glued as well, "hanging upside down, her bare feet attached to the living room's high ceiling." Confused and annoyed at first, he tries to peel her off but then gives up and sees the humor in the situation. "I laughed too. She was so pretty and illogical, hanging upside down like that from the ceiling. Her long hair falling down, her breasts poised like two drops of water under her white T. So beautiful." He then climbs on a pile of books in order to kiss her. "I felt her tongue touching mine, the pile of books pushed away from under me; I felt that I was floating in the air, touching nothing, hanging only by her lips."

The magical realism with which the story ends masks the more conventional and even conservative values it promotes of marital fidelity and constancy. Strangely, the beginning of the story feels like a throwback to earlier times, with the husband hurrying to work in the morning and the wife staying at home to do household chores. The mise-en-scène as well as the dialogue seem deliberately conventional, almost clichéd, including the husband's parting words, "It's already eight, . . . I must run," after which he picks up his briefcase and kisses her on the cheek, with the predictable addition, "I'll be home late today because . . ." These, as well as the row the couple has before that, somehow conjure up a 1950s American film, pastel colors and all. The only indication that it takes place in Israel is the Hebrew of the story and the mistress's name, Michal.

The fact that the happy ending of such optimistic films is realized by the end of the story through magic only heightens the pathos and deepens the longing for such solutions in the contemporary Israeli context.

This is true for the magical superglue as well, which is another meta-phor, forced, satirical, and problematic, perhaps, for the frustrating wish for clarity and stability. Placed at the end of a volatile anthology, then, "Crazy Glue" presents a solution of sorts that privileges permanency and especially love. The story also exhibits two major components of Keret's writing: the longing for the restoration of bourgeois values and the universal frame of references and imagery, especially from popular media, through which these values are manipulated and delivered. Sig-nificantly, the appellation "bourgeois" here is meant positively as a sign of stability, propriety, civility, etc., and not in the more derogatory sense it had in socialist-Zionist discourse. The final image of the story com-bines the two whimsically and eloquently by expressing reconciliation, unity, and the permanence of love through a common cinematic device, the "freeze frame."

This sense of isolation within the confines of a romantic relationship, unhinged from the immediate spatial and temporal surroundings, is much more pronounced in Keret's second anthology, *Missing Kissinger*, in which almost half of the stories deal with coupling. These stories abandon larger social or moral issues and instead retreat into the nar-rower, simpler limits of a one-on-one relationship, either with a pet, with a best friend, or more often with a woman. The narrator finds refuge from an incomprehensible world of disappearing borders, shifting mean-ings, and contradictory messages in the clear and simple allegiance he pledges to and demands from his immediate partners, and he derives his very reason for existence from the strength of these relationships.

The world in *Kissinger* is a violent world of disillusioned adolescents who grow up to discover that there are no dreams, that the relative safety of childhood is gone forever, and that life is in the gutter, to use a famil-iar Israeli phrase (החיים בזבל). The protagonists of the stories move be-tween nostalgia for the past—although this is often a problematic past, with broken homes and dysfunctional parents—and an attempt to find companionship, even if it is brief, sometimes with male friends but more often with a woman, with whom they hope to forge a special connection that will return a sense of stability, meaning, and belonging to their life.

The story "Corby's Girl," in which two guys vie for the same girl, con-veys this sense eloquently. At the beginning of the story the beautiful, tall, and blondish Marina dates Corby, a street thug (ערס). The uneven pairing is quizzical, especially to the narrator's brother, Miron, who eventually woos the girl away from Corby. Corby does not try to take his girl back, but he does punish Miron, at which point the story gets a little strange. "You stole my girl while I was still dating her," he yells at Miron, after beating him up with a crowbar and kicking him in the ribs. But then he does something that is less in keeping with his image and reputation. "Do you know," he says to Miron, "that there is a commandment against what you did? . . . It's called 'Thou shalt not steal.' But you, it flows by you like water." He then grabs Miron's brother and forces him to tell him what the Bible prescribes as punishment for violating that commandment. Fearing Corby's brutality, the brother refuses to comply but is finally tortured into saying it: "Death, I whispered. Those who violate it deserve to die." Satisfied, Corby lets go of the two and turns to his friend. Did you hear that? He says to him, "he deserves to die. And that, he pointed toward the sky, did not come from me but from the mouth of God. There was something in his voice as if he too was about to cry. Yalla, he said, let's go, I only wanted you to hear who is right."

Actual displays of love or romance barely if ever appear in this story, certainly not warm and compassionate expressions of them. Yet the story is one of Keret's most tender romantic stories in which love does conquer all. It subdues even a brutal thug like Corby, whose violence is really a searing expression of his heartfelt devotion to his lost girlfriend. Love elevates the uneducated, inarticulate Corby into a righteous judge and turns an idle bum into a moral and ultimately also a magnanimous being. Corby does not really think of his girlfriend as property that can be stolen. But he does subscribe to a rudimentary gentlemanly conduct, which Miron violates. Under these circumstances, Corby's vindication is perceived as both right and fair toward Miron, and touching toward Marina. Even Miron sees it at the end. Was it worth it, his brother asks him, now that she's with you? "Nothing in the world is worth that night," replies Miron, who confesses to his brother that he has been thinking a lot about Corby since then. Miron does not think Marina or any other girl is not worth the kind of hassle he went through. That's not it. He is extremely sorry for taking Marina away from Corby, for taking away his love. What he mourns at the end of the story is the demise of Corby's true love.

"Corby's Girl" is one of many romantic stories by Keret in which the quest for romance sorely fails, not just romance as we most often mean it about relationships between men and women, but also romance in the sense of a naïve belief in an idealized existence, like in the story "A Hole in the Wall" (*Chor bakir*). "On Bernadot Boulevard," begins the story, "right by the central bus station, there's this hole in the wall. . . . Someone told Udi once that if you shout your wishes into that hole in the wall, they come true." Although Udi doesn't believe it, he tries his luck one day and shouts into the wall that he wants Dafna to fall in love with him. The wish does not come true, but another one Udi made, to have an angel for a friend, does materialize. The angel, however, turns out to be a bit strange. He walks around with his wings folded under a big coat, refuses to fly, and seems altogether depressed. The two hang out together for a few years and seem to bond until one day Udi pushes the angel off the roof, "for kicks, he didn't mean anything bad by it, he just wanted to make him fly for a bit. . . . But the angel fell down five stories like a sack of potatoes" and splattered on the pavement below. Udi then realized that "nothing the angel ever told him was true; that he wasn't even an angel, just a liar with wings."

This story is romantic by inverse. Nothing in it is romantic except of course for its highly romantic premise. Udi's life is utterly devoid of romance. Like his friend the angel, he seems slightly depressed; someone without a purpose or joy in his life who leads a glum existence. It is surprising that Udi even bothers to go to the wall and shout into it because that would denote either gullible optimism or desperation, both of which Udi seems to lack or be beyond. More surprising still is what Udi wishes for, an angel, and that his wish actually comes true. But the most surprising thing of all is Udi's reaction at the end of the story, his shock and dismay not at the death of the man, but at the death of the angel. The real romantic core of the story is Udi's naiveté, his unrequited longing for a "miracle" even after years during which the magic slowly wears away by the continued exposure to life.

This desperate, pathetic, but very touching and also ironic quest is movingly suggested in another story, "Freeze!" (*Amodu!*), an ultimate adolescent male fantasy in which the protagonist manages to hook up with the most gorgeous women by exercising magical powers: when he shouts "Freeze!" everyone stops in their tracks and stands still. He is then able to go up to any girl he fancies, take her with him to his apartment, and have sex with her. But after his mother expresses some doubt as to the sincerity of these relationships, the troubled narrator stops doing it for a while and tries to date women in more conventional ways. But things don't work so well for him, and when one day he fails to woo a stunningly beautiful model he recognizes from a soft-drink ad, he cannot help himself and shouts "Freeze!" again. Now, the narrator realizes the difficulty he is in. Although he can keep the woman for as long as he wants, he would also like her to desire him for who he really is, not because she is compelled to do so. The solution comes to him in a flash: "I held her hand in mine, I looked her in the eyes and I said 'love me because of my character, because of who I really am.' Afterwards I took her back to my apartment . . . [and we had wild sex] . . . And she loved me, she really loved me because of who I really am."

In part, the focus of the romantic writers on relationships or love is the legacy of earlier trends that began in the 1960s, especially by female writers (Amalia Kahana-Carmon, Yehudit Hendel, Shulamit Hareven). Their cultivation of intimate interior spaces over the larger national and social engagement that characterized many of their male contemporaries slowly came to dominate Hebrew fiction since the 1980s. But these earlier texts by women that explored the economy of romantic relationships were still contextualized within a viable and discernible Israeli environment, even when they rebelled against it. What distinguishes the pursuit and attainment of love, or more precisely "couple-hood," in the narratives of the 1990s is not just a rebellion but a disengagement from a clearly identifiable Israel; a literary world that loses much of its local color in favor of elements borrowed from a more global culture. Love becomes chief among these elements not only because it insulates against a problematic Israeli present but also because of the central place it occupies in the lending culture, the popular culture of the West.

The hugely popular 1991 romantic novel *The Siren Song* (*Shirat ha-sirena*), one of the first pop or pulp fiction novels in modern Hebrew by journalist and pundit Irit Linur, can perhaps epitomize this development, all the more so because the novel is so trivial, an exaggerated example of a trend. Linur, who also began her career as a journalist in the country's emerging new private media, and who is sometimes included as one of the Lean Language writers, legitimized the trashy or pulp romance in Hebrew letters for the first time.[33] Pulp fiction was a label coined by Linur herself (she used the Hebrew *roman lemeshartot*, a maidservant's romance), who made fun of critics that tried to mine her work for deeper significance.[34] She openly admitted her intention to write a superficial work that had lots of sex in it, "because sex is simply not an option that exists in Hebrew literature."[35] The phenomenal success of Linur's home-grown Hebrew pulp is a telling indication of the profound changes Israeli society was undergoing at the time. Astute critics like Ariana Melamed were quick to recognize it. "*Siren Song*," wrote Melamed, "is a monumental breakthrough . . . a self-proclaimed disposable book that has no aspirations whatever. . . . Finally, we have real sex conducted in Hebrew." Other critics commended the novel for what it lacked, namely none of the usual Jewish-Israeli existential anxieties like the Holocaust, the Arab-Israeli conflict, or religious or ethnic tensions. The deficiency was lauded as a welcome rejection of the over-politicization of life and art in Israel while the excesses of romance, love, and sex were praised as the most addictive and satisfying junk, "wonderfully and completely entertaining." [36]

This is how the book begins:

> I received my frozen pies' account during the Rosenbaum-Marco New Year's party, as well as the undivided attention of Ronen Marco himself. I expected neither. Actually, I didn't expect anything at all. I came to the party so that, in addition to the reputation I already had as pushy and meddling, no one in the office would be able to say that it's beneath me to dance with them. There were limits to my willingness to take false abuse. That's why I decided to show up, with two caveats: first, I made sure to come after midnight, so that I won't get stuck with no one to kiss, or that, God forbid, I would have to kiss someone. Secondly, from the moment I entered, I made sure to minimize my presence as much as I could. I stood by the new Xerox machine and leaned against the glass brick wall that separated it from my office. That particular corner had its advantages, I could smoke there and if I really pressed against the wall, I could see Tzvika Rosenbaum dancing with his new secretary. There are things I simply cannot stand, not even in New Year's parties.

The hedonistic, consumerist, and inconsequential nature of this fluffy text, which continues apace until the very end of the novel, is self-evident. The marking of the secular new year, commonly referred to as Sylvester in Israel, identifies the secular, Westernized, and affluent milieu at the center of the book right away.[37] So does the location of the party, a Tel-Aviv advertising firm that forms the background to the story. All of these elements, delivered in a cool, detached, and cynical tone, convey a very new, a very different Israel; an Israel that is far removed from its ascetic beginnings; one that is more than a little European or American. Linur's characters are keenly aware of fashion brands, gourmet foods, contemporary as well as old films, and upscale vacation spots around the world.

But for the Scud missiles that rain on Tel-Aviv nightly, the Middle Eastern environment barely rears its inconvenient head. In fact, the heroine's most admired trait is her stubborn and oblivious pursuit of True Love, irrespective of the primitive and anachronistic conflict that rages around her, for which she has little patience and even less regard. Part of the novel's charm at the time was its refusal to acknowledge or deal with the complex Middle East situation and its insistence on having fun like the rest of the civilized world.

The initial excitement over Linur's works may sound strange to readers who are unfamiliar with the fervent ideologies that animated modern Hebrew literature since its beginnings in the nineteenth century. A cursory look at some of the histories of that literature, especially the last grand one by Gershon Shaked, can readily reveal such ideological fervor. Shaked's literary periodization is largely predicated on writers' commitment to Zionism—as is this study, for that matter. This is why Linur's complete disengagement from that literary tradition and her utter disregard for it struck readers and rang loudly in their ears like the defiant shout that opens Shalev's *Blue Mountain*.

Linur, much more so than Keret, abandons Zionism and Israel as points of reference in favor of wider world-cultural referents. She attenuates local politics in favor of deeper participation in an urban, Western, consumerist culture. Romance, love, and sex become the focus of this new culture for many reasons: they are not part of the Hebrew [literary] tradition; they constitute common human denominators that afford instant involvement and participation in other cultures; they encourage consumption of food, fashion, media, travel, and other goods; and as such they mark the pursuits of the privileged, the affluent, the discerning, a class Linur and her ilk felt they finally belonged to or ought to belong to after a long and forced abstinence.

It is easy to see the similarities between Linur's works and Keret's. The important difference, of course, was the degree of complexity with which these paradoxes were engaged and the deep pathos they conveyed. At his best, Keret wrote crisp stories that gave a precise voice to a tentative generation. His most impressive achievement was his ability to sound that voice in a new jargon, incorporating novel modes of expression in Hebrew that were not culled from ancient Jewish sources but rather from contemporary ones. His contribution in this regard was not universally appreciated. The most interesting condemnation of his style was his designation as *Palmachnik*, a reference to the first generation of native Israelis, known not only for their valor and dedication to the new state, but also for their linguistic revolution.[38] His cutesy street, army, and media argots were deemed cloying by some, who also did not appreciate the contempt for education, knowledge, and familiarity with the riches of the Israeli past that the generation as a whole displayed.[39]

One irony of these critiques is the hallowed place the PALMACH occupies today in Israeli history, constituting one of those very riches mentioned above. Another is the similar accusations that were leveled forty years before that at the *Palmachniks* or Sabras, who were men of action that spurned education and erudition, especially of the Jewish, traditional kind. Beyond that, such critiques miss one of the biggest anxieties of that literature. Keret may have written extremely brief texts that never delve too deeply into the wealth of issues they mention in passing, like a string of trailers that are never followed by an actual film.[40] But this is precisely what the string of trailers denotes—the absence of a film. This was precisely the problem. There was no film because there was no script, and there was no script because no one knew what to put in it and how to write it. This was the very sense of the generational vacuum that Yosef Al-Dror lamented.[41] Critics may have been annoyed at what they called Keret's contrived pose, at his smarmy linguistic imitations twice removed in which everything sounded so "groovy," like "two tourists stuck in a minefield."[42] But this is just how a young Israeli Generation X felt at the time, and Keret, better than most of his peers, gave that generation a small but very poignant voice.

The next chapter looks at the other romantic writers who did not deal as directly with the existential anxieties Keret handled, especially in his earlier stories. Although Gadi Taub, Uzi Weil, and Gafi Amir were shaped by many of the same forces that can be found in Keret's works and express many of his sensibilities, they explore the romantic option more exclusively in their writing and ensconce themselves even more in the urban bubble called Tel-Aviv.

Four   ROMANCE AS A DEFIANT
ESCAPE

If Etgar Keret expressed some of the main anxieties of his generation and suggested romance as an interim or temporary solution for the confusion of his age, Gadi Taub, Uzi Weil, and Gafi Amir developed this solution further. They also explored Israel's inexorable draw toward the urban, capitalist, and consumerist influences of the West which attended the age and loomed large over it. In fact, much of the confusion these writers evinced at the time stemmed from a gradual increase of these influences over life in a post-national Israel. But unlike popular culture in general (newspapers, television, popular literature), Taub, Weil, and Amir did not embrace these influences wholeheartedly and uncritically. Although most of their works consider romance as the central idiom of the new culture, they present it in nuanced ways that often seem patently unromantic. Their stories heave a deep and melancholy sigh of unrequited longing that comes from the friction between their romantic premise and the inability to realize it.

Each of the three writers explores a different aspect of the new life and times of the country through semantics of love, as it were. In his first [and so far only] collection of short stories, Gadi Taub isolates his heroes in quiet spaces by themselves where the only noise, save that of their own thoughts, is the faint call of possible love. Romance is explored much more dramatically and not always conventionally in Uzi Weil's first collection of short stories, "The Day They Shot the Prime Minister Down," whose parenthetical title is in fact "Love Stories." Finally, Gafi Amir's stories look at the nature of love as a commodity in a commercial age.

GADI TAUB

Gadi Taub's literary debut, like that of Keret, attracted media attention almost immediately after he published his 1992 collection of short stories, *Ma haya kore in hayinu shochachim et dov* (What Would Have Happened If We Forgot Dov).[1] The references to his work were not as prolific as the attention Keret received, but they were just as astute. "Taub," wrote Iri Rikin in the daily *Ma'ariv*, contemporizing older critiques of previous literary generations,

> is another link in a generation of Tel-Aviv journalist-writers who have recently emerged, including Etgar Keret, Irit Linur, Gafna Amir, and Uzi Weil. Simplistically speaking, what is common to all of them is a rejection of the literary Hebrew of the past and its substitution with a contemporary, spoken idiom that they use to create direct and unadorned prose. Another of their characteristics . . . is an almost complete disconnection from the weighty subjects that preoccupied their predecessors and their interest in personal matters and the existential anxieties of a local youth that could have probably been written in any other western metropolis.[2]

Rikin's appraisal was shared by other readers, all of whom wondered about the correspondence between what they called Taub's lean language and the equally spare emotive register of his stories. Avi Katz put it perhaps most perceptively when he identified Taub's penchant for metonymic fragmentation over a richer and more symbolic use of language as a way to de-mystify and negate hierarchies or centralizing ideologies.[3] Taub, he wrote, "democratizes reality, looks life in the eye and offers a very secular, very Tel-Avivite and unfocused way of interpreting the world." In other words, Taub's early short stories adumbrated the generational ennui which he elucidated much more clearly later on when he studied the period critically in his *Dispirited Rebellion*.

"Quiet desperation" is how Dan Miron described the silence that envelops the stories, their muted and seemingly oblivious observation of quotidian minutiae.[4] For Miron, Taub's terse texts do not indicate malaise or an unbaked literary talent that flaunts its cultural and linguistic ignorance and substitutes it with a contrived poetic stance.[5] Instead, the stories have a new and perhaps even a revolutionary role within the culture as an important voice in a growing choir that opposes the canon.

Young writers like Taub, wrote Miron, offer a resolute antithesis to the likes of Amos Oz, A. B. Yehoshua, Yehoshua Kenaz, and David Grossman, to their luxuriant style and to the national consciousness in which their works are steeped.

Miron noted that the opposition of non-hegemonic writers like Taub is not waged loudly and fiercely, like many of the generational wars that crowd the annals of Hebrew literature. But the soft and non-confrontational tones it strikes are still part of its dogged "platform" to undermine the regnant, national(istic) literary center. The most decisive aspect about Taub's heroes is not their age or their social or ethnic background but their dim and minimal consciousness. The meagerness of a seemingly depthless text that delivers slices of a banal life becomes an expression of an acute psychological disconnection. Rather than face their problems head on, these young men and women find refuge in inaction, floating in a severed and fragmented present.

These listless Israelis beg a comparison to one of their better-known literary predecessors, the *Talush* (lit. severed, meaning alienated here), a recurrent character in the literature of the Tehiya, the Hebrew Revival, at the beginning of the twentieth century. Both were young members of Jewish communities that underwent ideological crises and were poised at significant cultural crossroads. As a result, both also found themselves in an existential limbo that prevented them from going forward. But the similarities end here. The *Talush* of fin-de-siècle Hebrew literature may have been imprisoned by a paucity of existential opportunities that hemmed him in, but he compensated for his lack of freedom with an agitated and hyper-sensitive consciousness. It was a consciousness all too knowledgeable of the rich Jewish past and all too cognizant of the difficulties of molding a viable Jewish future out of its dated traditions. The lost sons of the Israeli middle class, as Miron calls Taub's heroes, faced the opposite problem about one hundred years later. As members of a privileged Jewish generation they seem arrested by a plethora of opportunities that render them numb and immobile.

But although they lack the angst of Keret's heroes, the generational identification of Taub's protagonists, as well as their age, their situation in life, the scope of their experiences, and even their life in Tel-Aviv, are sharper in his works. Taub's are much more muted stories whose silence comes from what Miron calls lack of soul, an inability to communicate with the world, which results in a mental stasis of sorts. But the narratives do not express a "quiet desperation." The sense of therapeutic lull, an almost healthy calm, and an atmosphere of convalescence are much stronger than desperation in the stories. It is apparent not only in the close and seemingly unconscious "cinematic" attentiveness to the smallest details—lighting up a cigarette, making coffee, lying in bed and staring into space—but in the direct and unornamented prose of these fragments. The descriptive dryness of the texts constitutes a palliative to a loud and busy literature whose protagonists are often verbose and over-conscious.[6] In Taub's stories the characters seem like recuperating patients in a sanitarium. Not a traditional sanitarium high in remote mountains somewhere, but in Tel-Aviv, a city without a past, built on Israel's most western sands. The characters in Taub's stories may not communicate too well or too keenly, but they do so out of choice, preferring to sit quietly by themselves and just "be" for a while, without a reason, without justification, without any of the intense anxiety and fervent consciousness that mark their literary precursors.

Such, for example, is the story "The Piano" (*Hapsanter*), in which the protagonist, Ariel, arrives at his brother's apartment in Tel-Aviv early one Saturday morning after running away from his army base. "There was no one in the streets. Down by the sidewalk water flowed toward the [Karmel] market and the rain kept coming down. Everything was quiet." For Ariel, the early morning silence in the streets, especially on the Sabbath, stands in blessed contrast to the pressure of the army life he escaped. The calm continues after he enters the apartment too, even after he confesses his absence without leave. "I ran away from the base," he tells his brother's girlfriend, Galia, who simply repeats it, "You ran away from the base."

> "Yes."
> "Now?"
> "Yes."
> "And they won't notice you're missing?"
> "They will in the evening, when they do roll call."
> "What will you do, then. . . . They'll catch you if you don't go back."
> Ariel shrugged his shoulders. "They won't be looking for me so quickly," he said.[7]

Ariel is never portrayed as a deserter, and his actions do not register as morally problematic with anyone in the story, including the narrator. Both his brother and his girlfriend treat it casually and at times even sympathetically. "You want to eat something?" Galia asks him. "There's rice in the fridge and there are hamburgers in the freezer." And when Ariel declines and says he wants to sleep, she simply notes, "You're tired," and says, "There are some blankets in a cardboard box under our bed and you can shut the door to the living room," accommodating him and giving him space.

The real reason for the desertion is revealed later on, when the brother returns and finds out that Ariel was punished severely for smoking on guard duty. For ten days he was forced to carry a forty-pound fire extinguisher everywhere he went, including during training. When there was no sign that the torture would ever end he ran away. "Sons of bitches," he says to his brother in a muffled voice, trying to hold back the tears. And the brother, who sympathizes and wants to help, tells him his own "war" story, how he too ran away from the army one time.

The story is obviously one-sided, told from Ariel's perspective. But, somehow, this is not important. Ariel's guilt or innocence is not the issue at all. The story does not really deal with it on any significant level. In fact, because of the stillness and calm that pervades the story, the army seems an aberration, a disruption of something much more precious: the soothing minutiae of everyday life. Details such as, "Galia took a plate with some chicken sections in it out of the refrigerator; she touched them to see if they thawed and then put them in a pot," gradually suffuse the story with tranquil domesticity. The great sense of a sabbatical peace that slowly descends on the story makes the army seem strange and faraway, a nuisance. The anticlimactic and inconclusive ending of the story underscores this even further. Neither the brother nor the girlfriend has words of wisdom for Ariel. It is up to him to find his way, which is fine, as long as he is left alone and allowed to contemplate it in peace. Like many of Taub's tenuous heroes, Ariel also stares symbolically out a window at the end: "After he finished [eating], he lit a cigarette and opened the kitchen shutters. [His brother's] Citroen stood on the sidewalk below the window, still wet from the rain." Ariel may be vague about the future, but he is uncompromising about the present. He may not know what he wants to be when he grows up, but he is absolutely certain that right now he wants to be left in peace.

An elaboration on this theme can be found in another story, "August," which literally deals with the restorative qualities of silence. Yonatan's tour of duty is cut short and he is released from the army for psychological reasons after he has a nervous breakdown. Yonatan's breakdown is unexplained.

> None of his army buddies could have guessed it was coming. Not even him. He was an ordinary soldier, fairly quiet, never

problematic, until suddenly, without warning, something happened to him. It happened early one morning, out on maneuvers. He woke up that night, silently put his uniform on and went out of the tent. On the way to the dining-room he buttoned his shirt. His rifle remained by his sleeping bag. The dining-room was empty and dark. It was a long tent with tables and wooden benches arranged in three rows. There were two long aisles between the rows that led to a screen that separated the soldiers' tables from those of the officers. A little before the screen there was an opening to the kitchen. Yonatan sat on one of the benches and put his palms straight in front of him on the table. After a moment, as if he thought better of it, he pulled them back again and remained leaning forward on his elbows. That's how the attendants on duty found him at five o'clock in the morning when they came in to set the tables. (52)

After he is diagnosed, Yonatan is sent to convalesce for a few weeks in a psychiatric ward and then released from service altogether. The story never dwells on his emotional reactions to any of this, but rather continues to follow him, factually recording his actions as he leaves the hospital, goes to live in Tel-Aviv, works at odd jobs, looks for rental apartments, and meets a girl he likes.

Since the text provides little explanation for any of these, meaning is derived from the gaps it creates, from the juxtaposition between the reported dry facts and the deeper significance they gather in the reader's mind. The first three sentences of the excerpt above constitute the narrator's only direct acknowledgment of the seriousness or consequence of the event. The breakdown was a surprise to everyone, even for Yonatan, which is perhaps the oddest thing about it. A nervous breakdown is usually the result of a long psychological process. It does not occur in a vacuum. It is typically provoked by external factors that cause mounting levels of stress. So the fact that Yonatan showed no warning signs of the approaching breakdown is odd and bears mention. All the more so, since Yonatan was an ordinary, quiet soldier who never had problems before.

The rest of the excerpt is devoid of qualifiers and is much more in keeping with the peculiar nature of the event, especially with the disconnection that Yonatan experiences from his immediate environment. Despite the dramatic opening, the narrator never dwells on the crisis Yonatan underwent in the sentences that follow. He simply provides a factual record of his actions as if he were looking at him through the lens of a camera. Rather than use omniscience, the narrator assumes the neutrality of an aperture, observing Yonatan without commenting on what he does or taking us into his head. He oddly records, though, how "on the way to the dining-room [Yonatan] buttoned his shirt." There is nothing odd of course about the action itself. The incongruity comes from the particular placement of the "recorded" segment in the text. The reader is eager to find out about Yonatan's mental state, to know how he feels right now and to see signs of his agitation. But all we get is yet another factual and ostensibly neutral record.

The entire passage is constructed from such impartial observations that seem to bear little on the significance of the event. We are told that Yonatan leaves his rifle behind and next, the dining room is described for no apparent purpose. We were never told that Yonatan was going there. Then, even more time is spent on a fairly detailed account of the dining room's layout. By now we are even more anxious to know specifics about Yonatan's mental health, but instead we focus on the contours of the dining room, we learn that it is long, that it has wooden tables and benches arranged in three rows, that it has two aisles. We know where the officers sit. We know where the kitchen is. The only thing we are still not told is how Yonatan feels. Yet we know it nevertheless. We understand the severity of his confusion, his inability to relate to anything around him from the odd collection of fragments that record his actions. The gap that is created here—noting the ordinary action in lieu of more comprehensive information—actually stresses the acuteness of Yonatan's mental breakdown. The incongruent text that offers little correspondence between the facts it records and their significance provides a literal mimesis of the mental disturbance Yonatan experiences without describing it in so many words.

Yonatan's inability to negotiate his surroundings coherently and understand himself makes sense in his disrupted psychological condition. His inability to do so before, however—to be aware of his mental state, to realize that something is seriously wrong with him and "guess that [the breakdown] was coming"—does not make as much sense. Yet the text correlates the two—Yonatan's state of consciousness before the breakdown and after it. The relatively long record of the soldier's random actions after he breaks down is applied in retrospect to his consciousness before he collapsed. The result is a young man whose self-awareness is very limited, the kind of young man with the minimal consciousness Miron describes.

This is the way the story begins. Throughout the rest of it, Yonatan literally takes time off to get better. From the army, he is sent to a psychiatric ward in a hospital, where he spends a few weeks in total silence and where no one bothers or pressures him. He is left alone and slowly gets better. "A week after he came to the hospital he started eating by himself. . . . After about three weeks, when Yonatan began to talk again, it became apparent that he was aware of what was going on around him for a few days now." Yet all this time he never blames anyone. He never gets angry or frustrated. He is strangely calm, asking short and very basic questions. "The first thing he wanted to know is what happened to him." But when the doctor explains to him, "Yonatan looked at his lips and then stared at the window." He is peculiarly uninvolved, uninterested even. "When can I go?" he asks simply, and when the doctors confirm that he was discharged from the army altogether he quietly repeats the words and looks out the window again. He does not even emote when the doctors gingerly tell him that his parents know everything. When the doctors leave,

> Yonatan got out of bed. He stood barefoot on the floor and
> looked at his feet. The floor was cool. He moved his toes.
> Then he went over to the window, opened it and looked out-
> side. The remote sound of the sprinklers on the lawn by the
> entrance was barely audible. Apart from the sprinklers, there
> was a pleasant silence. He thought of calling his parents
> and tried to think what he'd tell them, but the cool floor
> felt good on his feet and he remained by the window. Then
> he sat on the floor and leaned against the wall. It wasn't too
> hot outside and the light breeze blew air under the loose
> hospital shirt. Yonatan closed his eyes and leaned his head
> backwards. (56)

These are not the actions of a quietly desperate man but those of someone who slowly wakes up to the world around him after a long sleep or absence, or like the actions of a sick man who is slowly recovering and cautiously tests the limits of his renewed strength. Rather than confront his parents and be dragged into an emotional confrontation—the doctor told him that his father took the breakdown harshly—Yonatan prefers to postpone it. Eventually, he avoids it altogether. If Yonatan has rejected the army somehow, turned away from what it represents for Israelis, abandoned it as a national rite of passage, he never does so with fore-thought, intent, or passion. It simply happens, like the breakdown, and

Yonatan does not mull over it. The astounding thing about it, of course, is Yonatan's indifference. Military service ceases to have any significance, national or even personal. Yonatan simply drops it one day, as if it were an empty wrapper. His mother's tears and his father's displeasure at the news are the only reminders that the service ever mattered, that it had any significance. But Yonatan does not even bother to confront them, excuse himself, apologize, or expend any energy on the matter whatever. From the hospital he goes directly to his sister, who "asked nothing about what happened or about their parents." Thus begins Yonatan's slow and silent recovery, first at his sister's apartment and then, after a few weeks, in a rented apartment in Tel-Aviv.

Yonatan's mental history takes up a small part of the story. The rest of it unfolds in extraordinary silence as Yonatan makes symbolically languid attempts to find another apartment after his lease runs out. Here, too, the slow and lazy search is peculiar because Yonatan has only a week to find a new place. Yet he strolls through Tel-Aviv as if he had all the time in the world, unconcerned with his deadline, with the small number of available apartments, and with the fact that he may not even be able to afford those. Just as in the army and in the hospital before that, Yonatan is oddly indifferent to what goes on around him, or better yet, conducts the search almost as if he were a tourist in his own life. Sometimes his indifference seems to come from an inner peace and at other times from a conscious decision to shut out the outside world and focus internally instead.

That he is clearly selective in his responses to outside stimuli becomes apparent from his reaction to a renter in one of the apartments he visits, a young woman whose "quiet but clear" voice strikes him. Compared to his numbness before, Yonatan comes to life after meeting the woman. His attraction to her is not conceded outright by his descriptions of her or by intimations of his feelings toward her. When she opened the door, Yonatan "felt confused for a second. That's not how he pictured her to himself." He "was sorry he didn't dress better and shave." He then becomes animated and conversational and later that day suggests they look for apartments together. "There was a chance they'd find a two-bedroom apartment that would be good for both and they could rent it together. He wasn't going to suggest it outright. But it could still happen. In any case, even if it didn't, he could maybe keep in touch with her, or at least know where she lived." This is the first time in the story Yonatan takes initiative. Letting his thoughts run away with him, he decides that after their visit to the realtor's office tomorrow he would invite her for lunch at his apartment.

He closed his eyes. He liked the lunch idea. He laid down
some more and then got up, dressed and went over to the
supermarket by Ben-Yehuda cinema. He bought meat, and
rice, and oil, and vegetables, and white wine, and two coke
bottles. On his way out, after paying, he remembered that
he needed lemon for the salad and he went back in. Inside,
he also bought salami and humus. (66)

The author never confides to the reader any of his hopes about the
woman, but they are obvious from his careful planning, which he
continues energetically at home. Although he had already packed his
belongings and put everything in boxes, he unpacks everything and
rearranges his apartment so it would feel cozier for tomorrow's lunch.
He works until one o'clock in the morning, and although "his body felt
tired he was still wide awake." This is the first time in the story Yonatan
takes such an active interest in life; the first time he is alert. At the end,
Yonatan does not get the girl. They have a nice lunch together and they
vaguely promise to stay in touch, but when he calls her up two days later,
he finds out that she is gone.

Like many of the protagonists in Taub's stories, Yonatan is a modern
talush, a young man who is in search of a life, although, significantly,
not necessarily meaning. He lives or rather exists alone, but he is not
lonely. He craves solitude, silent moments that would allow him to hear
himself. Yonatan and his other literary contemporaries are not necessarily tuning in to listen to their own thoughts. Often, their minds are
blank. Their biographical information is minimal, they have only immediate family or none at all, they have few friends, they have little or no
past, they live in an ongoing present. This is a programmatic isolation,
a poetic stance mounted in opposition to the over-involvement of more
canonical works. And since the canon is conceived by the romantic writers as false and hollow, they have little interest in challenging it directly.
Such opposition would not only acknowledge its value, it would also em-
broil them in its distasteful politics.[8] Instead they turn to romance as a
solution of sorts.

Yonatan in "August" is hardly a romantic. But he leaves the cocoon he
ensconced himself in only after meeting a girl. The chance for a romantic relationship is the only stimulus that has any effect on him, the only
outside sound that penetrates the filter he has put around him. Meeting
the girl does not open him up to the world and does not make him take
more of an interest in it. The girl alone interests him. He no doubt hopes

to love her as well. But once that chance slips away he returns to his former daze. After he finds out the girl is gone, Yonatan stares blankly into space, thinking how "he'd need to pack everything up again in the boxes. . . . In the meantime he remained sitting on the floor, leaning against the wall under the big window. A little later," concludes the story, "when his sister tried to call, he was still sitting there. The phone rang next to him, but he didn't pick it up."

Relationships, love, romance, or hopes for them constitute the few meaningful points of contact the characters in Taub's stories have with the world around them. These young men and women establish communication with a world they intentionally shut out only when they perceive in it a chance for romance, even if it is vague or noncommittal. The point is not durability or longevity but the kind of contact, a soulful connection that must have a measure of love in it. The pattern repeats itself in many of the stories, even those in which the protagonists are married, as in the story "Stitches" (*Tfarim*) about a married man who falls in love with a waitress and romantically courts her. Infidelity is not an issue in the story, not just because it ends before the two have sex. The story is devoid of a moralistic center. Even the injury which the husband's little daughter sustains, ostensibly as "punishment" for her father's transgression, leaves him strangely distant. Sitting in the hospital with her as she gets stitched, he looks on as she screams and wonders "how such small vocal cords can produce such powerful sounds . . . The doctors had to scream in order to hear each other. I never heard such screams. I don't understand how anyone can stitch in this noise."

The protagonist is a dutiful husband and an attentive father. He pays attention to his wife and takes care of his little girl, but he seems distant from them, disengaged. He comes to life only after his infatuation. The waitress awakens something dormant in him, which is why he pursues her, even though "I knew I'd regret what I'm doing." He continues to perform his marital duties and does so conscientiously, but all the while he is thinking of Michal, the waitress. Driving his daughter back home after a day of fun in the city, he turns on the car radio and starts to sing. "I sang loudly on purpose and it amused [my daughter] and made her laugh. At one of the stoplights I took off my coat. The cool breeze felt nice. Then we stopped at a flower stand. I bought a bouquet and on the way home I passed through Michal's place. I left [my daughter] in the car for a moment and went up. But I didn't knock on the door. I just placed the bouquet on the floor with my name on a note." The maintenance of two different worlds simultaneously, held together by crude and temporary "stitches," as Miron writes, without apparent awareness of the conflict or its toll, demonstrates dim consciousness indeed. At the same time, the surge of vigor that the protagonist feels after his infatuation is, on balance, a welcome respite from his emotional barrenness.

It is not surprising, of course, that Taub's stories and those of other First Person Dual writers deal with relationships. These were, after all, stories about young people in their twenties written by young people in their twenties who think a lot about dating. The surprising aspect about the stories is actually the lack of sex in them. Despite the heroes' young age and the fact that most of them are single and lead a pretty free life in a Western metropolis, sex is conspicuously absent. Instead, almost all of the stories have an old-fashioned and decidedly romantic bend to them. This is true even of one of the few stories that actually mentions sex, and a lot of it.

No'am in the story "What Would Have Happened If We Forgot Dov" is quietly attracted to his beautiful neighbor, a young married woman who has moved into his apartment building with her husband and their baby. Another of Taub's silent and inactive heroes, who passively observe the world from a perch, No'am eventually has a hushed but torrid affair with his neighbor. The two sneak into each others' apartments at odd times of the day and night and have hot, passionate sex. But when No'am catches his neighbor one day having casual sex with someone else in her apartment, a handyman, he is shocked. No'am "remained standing in the hallway and breathed deeply through his mouth to avoid being heard. He waited to hear if she would say something, and only after he was sure she wasn't going to he turned around quietly toward the door . . . and realized he'd have to move out."

The love affair here, like in "Stitches," is not depicted as betrayal but is told with the same direct dryness that characterizes the stories in general. No'am expects his neighbor to be faithful to him in a way, not because he is a chauvinist but because he is in love with her. For him, the affair is not meaningless, and when the powerful draw he feels toward his neighbor is not reciprocated, he feels betrayed. The clandestine sex the two have does not cheapen their connection. It adds to its significance and sanctions it. This is why the romantic No'am feels deceived and why he wants to leave when he finds out that the woman does not "love" him exclusively, her husband notwithstanding. Instead of a contemptible philanderer, No'am appears as an endearingly innocent and wide-eyed romantic. Instead of furtive and dirty, sex in the story intensifies the romance. It builds it up and then perpetuates it by making it untenable and unrequited.

To say that Taub's characters lead undramatic lives would be an understatement. As their outlines are drawn with a very light pen, so are their loves. Romance does not help any of them in any significant or life-altering ways. At most it provides a temporary relief from their emotional numbness and makes them feel again, connect with the world around them. These are not substantial connections, but ones that are limited in scope, directed at the object of affection. But in the desert that is around them, these romances provide a meager shade, a vague promise, a distant chance for refuge and perhaps meaning.

UZI WEIL

The use of romance in Uzi Weil's short stories is more pronounced and much more dramatic, often even melodramatic, and certainly closer to the play it usually received in more popular media. His first collection of short stories, *Bayom shebo yaru berosh hamemshala* (The Day They Shot the Prime Minister Down),[9] reminded some critics of popular detective stories, only instead of suspenseful narratives, Weil spun narratives of sentiment, "stories that attempt to . . . touch the exposed nerve of love and its addictive and destructive power."[10] Less favorable critiques of Weil's populist tendencies faulted him for an excess of romance and sentimentalism.[11] This was not an uncommon reading of the stories. Even those who liked them and credited Weil for his convincing descriptions of sex, for instance—a Hebrew literary rarity indeed—noted his occasional syrupy slips, as they called it.[12] But there were those who already then identified the angst below the sentimentalism: "What remains after the disappointment, the burping and the masturbation is a beat-up life waiting for the forgiving promise of a wholesome love."[13] Weil, continued the same critic, achieves the right balance between sex and emotion and washes "the filth of life with the redemptive act of love."

Uzi Weil admitted many of these attributes a priori when he subtitled his anthology *Sipurey ahava* (Love Stories). The parenthetical title itself was somewhat unusual, because, as I already mentioned in the introduction, save for a few exemplary instances (Agnon), Hebrew literature has seldom engaged with the subject to any meaningful extent. Canonical literature was especially mum about it. The very composition of the stories and their compilation under the sign of "Love," then, was unusual. Here was a serious, high-brow literature borrowing from more popular, lower-brow literature. It is likely that the composition of love stories and their designation as such acknowledged the influence of popular media by integrating one of its central idioms. Given the novelty and proliferation of these new venues in Israel at the time, there is little wonder that Weil, as well as other contemporary writers, was influenced by it. At the same time, Weil uses this idiom in innovative ways that go beyond the banal and ubiquitous forms it receives in Hollywood films and American television shows. For Weil, love is both a cheap device and a way to comment on its cheapness. The stories place love and romance at the center as an organizing principle. But they also expose the irony of doing so in a culture that seems devoid or incapable of it. Weil, in other words, is a cynical romantic.

At his least successful moments, Weil could definitely sound gushing and sentimental, as in the story "Chayim kim'at metukim" (An Almost Sweet Life): "Liora grew up with a definite notion that something good will come her way; better than good, something big; something her heart was meant for and that was always just around the corner. She felt that the air was filled with hidden diamonds, only she could not find any of them just yet." The story's central idiom is that love is actually a country in which a person needs to be naturalized. "[Liora] had men, not many men, each of them different from the other. They were so different that I thought she was wandering in the world of love from country to country in order to find out which country would best suit her as a homeland."

At his best, though, Weil could be very subtle and use love in intricate and novel ways to comment not just on the variations of this ubiquitous sentiment but also on some of its more far-reaching implications. Such for example is his finest and longest story in the collection, "Bekarov yikre lecha mashehu tov" (Something Good Will Happen to You Soon). The elaborate core of the story is framed by a simpler exterior narrative. Both stories are predicated on the absence and craving for love, although each of them deals with it on different levels and has something very different to say about love. The exterior story is about Ilan, a young teenager who runs away from a loveless home to join his sister in Tel-Aviv. The sister is estranged from the family because of a relationship she had with an Arab, whom she wanted to marry until he left her. Gradually, the brother and sister become sexually involved, until Ilan is caught up in the internal story that puts an abrupt end to it. The perverted love between the brother and the sister is used not only as a comment on the absence of love both felt at home. It is also a counterpoint to the melodramatic love affair of the sister and the Arab. Before running away,

Ilan was angry and ashamed at the way his parents treated his sister and, to relieve his rage, "he read again the first letters in which Dalia wrote about her love for Yassar, when they were still together. . . . How they ate together and drank and went to movies and danced in discotheques and how he told her he loved her and she told him that she loved him too." As Ilan sees it, Yassar may have left his sister, but at least she experienced true love.

The storybook qualities of this inter-ethnic romance are undermined by the brother's physical attraction to his older sister and her silent acceptance and eventual encouragement of him. If the hopelessness of the Jewish-Arab love story were not enough, Weil adds incipient incest as an additional contradiction. The perfect love between Dalia and Yassar is undermined by the imperfect love between Dalia and her brother. One love story provides an idyllic vision, the other a gross distortion of it. Love is put before us as a model for emulation but not as something that can survive real life. Weil the romantic promises love; Weil the cynic doubts it.

The inner story is much more involved and manipulates romanticism very differently. While he is staying with his sister, Ilan befriends an elderly neighbor, Avraham, a diehard communist who fought in the Spanish Civil War in the 1930s and then in Israel's Independence War. Avraham, in fact, is a character from an earlier story in the anthology, who moved away from a kind of urban commune he lived in because he fell in love with the young woman who ran it. On a very literal level, then, Avraham is a consummate romantic: he loves a woman passionately but sacrifices his love for her because he knows it is impossible. Moreover, his reappearance in a subsequent story in the same collection magnifies his irrepressible romanticism by extending it beyond his initial literary life span, as it were, and resurrecting it in another story.

But Avraham's romanticism extends deeper and farther than women. He is in point of fact a walking relic of a bygone era, an old-guard communist, a true believer, still extant, in the *Liberté, égalité,* and *fraternité* of the century's earlier revolutions. He derides what he considers the rampant corruption of Zionist ideals and still hopes to prove the superiority of his own. As far as he is concerned, Ben-Gurion "was a big criminal, a very big fascist. Communists like me couldn't say a word back then or they would be thrown into prison on some pretext." And when Ilan asks him if he is still a communist and what he thinks of Israeli communists today, Avraham dismisses them as ridiculous and effete.

"They don't know how to hold a rifle or make bombs out of empty cans; they don't know how to lay an ambush or blow up a bridge. . . . No one is afraid of them at all."

Avraham's obstinate belief in a better world, his smoldering anger about the defeat of his ideals, and his expertise as a military sapper, come to an explosive conclusion at the story's end. With Ilan at his side, he fortifies himself in an old, decrepit Tel-Aviv house slotted for demolition, booby-traps the place, and raises the red flag over it, ready to defend his old ideals to death. His wish for a last heroic stand is granted when the authorities converge on the house and try to remove him, first gingerly and then by mounting force. Avraham, however, is well prepared and exacts a painful and costly price from the illustrious Israeli army before he goes down. Because the narrator has been entrenched inside the urban redoubt together with Avraham and Ilan, the Israeli army outside becomes The Enemy, while the two comrades assume the righteous morality of desperados. Their fight is made all the more romantic because it is doomed.

Both Avraham and Ilan are complete and desperate romantics. Inspired by his sister's sweet love affair, Ilan leaves his home in search of love in his own life. That he does not find it, or rather experiences a distorted version of it, is the fault of his warped relations with his parents at home. On a much grander level, Avraham's life is animated by a similar dynamic. He too is inspired by ideals, specifically those of Communism, which he pursued throughout his life and which always eluded him. Avraham's loss finally takes its toll and makes him into a crazed "jihadist" just as Ilan's anxious thirst for love thrust him into the arms of his sister. In both these complementary stories love is used as a metaphor. It provides the vision as well as its dissolution or corruption.

The ludicrous Avraham is a reminder of an original promise as well as a witness to its dissipation. His Communism does not necessarily allude to a concrete political ideology as much as it marks some of the main qualities that are associated, especially in literature, with its ardent adherents, like idealism, loyalty, and resolve. In the greater context of the times, the early 1990s, the original promise is Zionist ideology. Its demise is the country's gradual betrayal of these ideals. While Avraham's story is an allegory about the past, Ilan's youth, naiveté, and great thirst for love represent a future promise. The tragedy, of course, is that the fate of both is bound together. Ilan's present inability to find a good and proper love stems partly from the wrongs that Avraham recounts and represents. Both men express Weil's passionate romanticism. But while the older man stands for the power and destructiveness of ideals, the younger signifies the value of love and its potential to transcend them.

The inner, fundamental conflict between these two poles is extended far more in Weil's less belletristic writings, for which he is better known: humoristic contributions to popular venues like *Ha'ir* and popular television shows like *The Chamber Quintet* and *The Strip* (*Haretsu'a*). Throughout most of the 1990s, after Yosef Al-Dror quit the paper, Weil composed the *Back Cover* of *Ha'ir* and made it wildly popular, a prodigious cultural icon.[14] Unlike Al-Dror, whose humor tended toward the existential, Weil's witticisms were more politically and socially grounded. He took Al-Dror's keen sense of the absurd and applied it more closely to contemporary Israeli life to create a refined cultural critique in the venerable tradition of Monty Python. Weil's nonsense was edgy and often daring. He stopped at nothing and subjected everything to his pointed pen, including the Holocaust and dead Israeli soldiers, two of Israel's most sacred taboos. Considering the decidedly romantic streak he shows in his short stories, then, Weil's brilliant but acerbic humor makes him a complex figure indeed.

Consider for instance the following dialogue, which appeared in the *Back Cover* of *Ha'ir* following the deadly suicide bombing attack in the Tel-Aviv shopping mall, Dizzengoff Center, in March of 1996:

The Limits of Good Taste (A) [15]

—Shalom, are you Ronit?
—Are you Shmulik?
—No, but Shmulik told me about you. He said there'd be a Ronit here.
—I'm not Ronit. I'm Hagit. Ronit told me about this blind date, but since she didn't feel like going . . .
(a conversation between an attractive young man and a good looking, young woman that was overheard by a suicide bomber from the Hamas who sat next to them in the café and tried to blow himself up, but his battery was dead. He turned to the man and asked: "Say, which is it, minus to plus or plus to minus?" The young man replied: "Minus to plus. It's always minus to plus, otherwise there's no closed electrical circuit. Didn't you go to school?" "It was closed by your army, when I was in third grade," said the suicide bomber

and continued to play with the wires. And this is only chapter A. Just wait and see the suspense in chapter B.)

The Limits of Good Taste (B)

—So, where were we? I understand you are a kindergarten nurse?
—No, Ronit is, I am a stewardess.
—Really? Air or ground?
—Sales.
—Seriously? I went shopping yesterday!
—Really? That's so interesting! (a continuation of the conversation between the attractive man and the fetching girl, which could have ended in a wedding, only the suicide bomber interrupted again and asked the man: "Pardon me, sir, I connected the minus to the plus, but—nothing. Why doesn't it work?")

"Excuse me for just a moment," said the striking man and picked up the wires that dangled from the bomber's body. "Who sold this to you?" he demanded.

"A soldier," said the bomber, "he needed money to operate on his mother the whore."

"Hey, don't you talk like this about soldiers."

"No, she was really a whore," explained the terrorist, "the operation was for a sex change."

"I see, that's O.K. then," said the alluring man and explained:

"Look, this charge is shit, there's no connection here."

"So what do I do?" asked the bomber.

"How do you Arabs say," the man shrugged his shoulders, "*Anna Arref* [how should I know], use a conductor here, maybe a fork."

And the single, attractive girl fluttered her eyelids at the man and said: "Wow, you really know a lot about electricity."

The Limits of Good Taste (Last chapter)

—Hey, do you want to have sex?
—Actually . . . look, Shmulik described Ronit to me, and from what she told him about herself there were supposed to be big tits. What about you?

—Well, I don't think I want to either. Ronit described
Shmulik to me and I was convinced he had a sex organ.
—I'm sorry, it's because of That War.[16]
—The Holocaust?
—No, the Lebanon War.
—Oh, well, then . . .
(and just when the terrorist was ready to say *Allah hu Akbar*
they picked up and left. The bomber became really upset,
and I wouldn't have mentioned the whole thing if the secretary of a prominent publicist hadn't called me that evening
to invite me to take part in a symposium about: "The Limits
of Good Taste in the Local Media.")

The deadly attack—thirteen killed and over a hundred wounded—in one
of the bastions of a bourgeois, secular Israel shook a country not yet used
to this kind of tactic; to the entry of the conflict with the Palestinians into
its own living room, as it were. In light of this, the tenor of Weil's piece
seems shocking. No one escapes unscathed in this ferocious sendup of
The Situation (המצב), as Israelis call their abnormal, Middle Eastern life
with its violent upheavals. Weil pokes vicious fun at the young couple and
potential victims of the imminent suicide attack. Both the man and the
woman are nonsensical creatures, vapid, self-centered, and completely
disconnected from what is going on around them: the young Israeli actually tries to assist the hapless Palestinian to discharge the explosive.

But the bodies that Weil hangs on the gallows of his humoristic pen
are far more numerous. His portrayal of the young couple is not only
critically defiant of the media's sanctimonious obituaries of such victims. The young people are also presented as mindless consumers of
goods ("I bought some products yesterday! / Really? That's so interesting!"), and as people who are incapable of real, meaningful connections.
They date each other and talk about themselves as if they were products:
"—Shmulik described Ronit to me, and from what she told him about
herself there were supposed to be big tits. / Ronit described Shmulik to
me and I was convinced he had a sex organ." Sex is casual and it is only
"sold" if the customer is pleased with the product. Both the man and the
woman speak of their own organs as if they were featured in a buyer's
catalogue. They also pretend to care about the Israeli army, one of the
last "sacred cows" of Israeli culture. The young man is quick to warn
the Arab not to disrespect soldiers. But his equally speedy acceptance of
the terrorist's explanation—"she was really a whore"—is specious. The

suicide bomber is brutally cut down as well. His ridiculous inanity plays on the jingoistic conventions of portraying Arabs in Israeli media and literature as fools and buffoons. But his ignorance veils a political accusation: Israel's frequent disruptions of life in the occupied territories, that is, its oppression of the Palestinians, breed ignorance and terrorism.

Is "Uzi the journalist," then, "an almost opposite mirror image of Weil the writer," as one critic wrote? [17] I am not so sure. Both of Uzi Weil's personas seem animated by a similar impulse. Irrespective of Rabin's assassination a few months prior to the Dizzengoff Center attack and the heavy blow it gave to the peace process he nursed, many Israelis still believed in 1996 in the promise of the Oslo Peace Accords to change the Middle East fundamentally. They were also buoyed by a sturdy economy and what appeared as the world's renewed reception of the country into its fold as a worthy, responsible member. Weil seems to be a staunch believer in these new opportunities, especially the chance for a true, civil Israeli society. His acerbic humor is predicated on a romantic's belief in his ability to change the world, to make a difference. His is not a cynical pen. His laugh is not a demonic cackle. The two sides of Uzi Weil do not conflict but rather complement each other. While his satire exposes the dangers of living a disconnected life in Israel, especially in the bubble called Tel-Aviv, his more literary creations suggest how to connect anew. Instead of the old, decrepit paradigm, Weil, like other First Person Dual writers, offers new ones, among which love is central.

"Make love not war" is indeed one of the group's most pervasive paradigms, as clichéd as it may sound, especially for Weil. What is less clichéd about it is the Israeli context, which lends this slogan subversiveness. Since Israel's wars were always presented by the country's political and ideological leadership as existential, and because they were perceived as such by most Israelis, undermining this perception challenged some of the nation's most fundamental beliefs. Weil's was not just the voice of political opposition, as in the case of the anti-establishment sentiments that originated the slogan in the United States in the 1960s. His was a rejection of a received Zionist truth about The Conflict; a narrative that was inculcated to generations of Israelis about their fight with the Arabs, and the military cult that it spawned.

"Ve'ata tihye met" (And You'll Be Dead), which opens the anthology, demonstrates this almost symbolically. The story begins in Oslo, Norway, where the protagonist, Edry, has been living unapologetically with a Norwegian woman for the past five years. A chance meeting there with his first girlfriend, Anat, takes him back to the winter of 1972, when he was still in the army, when Anat broke up with him, and when he had seen snow for the first time in his life. At one of the lowest points during his time in the army, Edry remembers, lonely and dejected in a remote base, late at night, his commanding officer brings him a letter from his girlfriend. The hated commander, jokingly perhaps, demands thirty pushups from Edry to redeem the letter. "His hand was holding the letter," Edry remembers,

> and on the envelope was her handwriting. After almost a
> year in the army, Anat was the only thing in my life that
> was still pure and sweet like I once wanted my life to be, the
> only thing worth getting up for in the morning and work
> another day. Her letter in his hand was the closest thing to
> sacrilege that a secular man like me can imagine. (11)

Edry refuses to comply and when the commander persists Edry loads his rifle, points it at him, and threatens to shoot. The enraged commander has no choice. He promises court-martial but hands over the letter, in which Anat tells Edry she wants to break up with him. In the end, the trial never materializes. On the day it is scheduled, heavy snows cut the base off from the rest of the world, and as they melt so does the complaint against Edry. Nature itself, it seems, intervened on behalf of the lover, rewarded him for his true love, and mended his broken heart.

GAFI AMIR

If Keret was a musketeer, as one early critic called him, Gafi (Gafna) Amir was a cowboy. This was, in fact, how she described herself in a conversation about her fourth published work, the collection of short stories, "By Age 21 You Will Reach the Moon." [18] "I saw all these people in Tel-Aviv pretending and striking poses (פלצנות ואֲוֶנטוֹת)," she told an interviewer, "so I felt like confronting them and giving it to them (אביא להם בקוֹנטרה), like some kind of upright cowboy." [19] Actually, Amir can be more accurately described as a combination of a cowboy and a damsel in distress, to use Western imagery again. The irony of both metaphors was Amir's impressive résumé. Not just her early writing for various youth magazines or her first novel, published before she was twenty-one, but her subsequent claim to fame: her authorship of an innovative and popular gossip column for the local Tel-Aviv weekly, *Tel-Aviv*. [20]

It was Amir's gossip column, titled "Not Really" or "In Jest" (סתם), and not her more serious journalism and her early attempts at belles lettres that got her first noticed.[21] Although Israel had gossip columnists before, most notably the gossip column of the anti-establishment paper, *Ha'olam Haze*, Amir changed some of the genre's rules when she began her column.[22] Although she supplied the required information about celebrities, parties, and openings, she did so with a decidedly satirical twist, making fun, in fact, of the very events and people she was supposed to gaze at with admiration. The traditional function of gossip in the media is certainly aimed at satisfying readers' voyeuristic interests. But it also confers an elevated status on its subjects, it recognizes them, and widens the gap between them and the ordinary, "mortal" readers. Amir, on the other hand, exposed the celebrities she wrote about as pretentious and presented the events they all went to as absurd, a vanity fair. She took an inherent but minor aspect of the genre, magnified it, and made it the central feature of her reporting.

Amir's innovation worked, and worked well. The column was extremely popular both with readers and, less intuitively, with celebrities themselves, who longed to make its pages. "The Tel-Aviv of Gafi Amir," read one report, may be "a city of impossible bullshitting (חרטוטים)," but its gossip items "function as national metaphors, whereby the shoe size of a famous model becomes part of the nation's ethos."[23] The reporter makes fun of Amir and the seriousness with which her column is taken. But his assessment also exposes the degree to which a capitalist revolution was sweeping Israel at the time. Amir's critical agenda notwithstanding, her gossip column recorded the rapid increase in the standard of living in Israel. Moreover, the popularity of a column about the fashion and lifestyle of the Israeli rich and famous was an indirect but very real evidence of a new consumerist society. It documented the existence of a growing number of Israelis who could afford to consume, who wanted to consume, who thought they knew what, how, and where to consume, and an even greater number of people, readers, who craved that information and aspired to the same.

The "cowboying" posture came from Amir's subversion of the genre. Instead of providing a pedestal for the new class of celebrities bred by the surging economy—models, television personalities, owners of fashionable boutiques, purveyors of trendy parties—she publicized their vainglory. She "gave it to them," as she put it, like a righteous cowboy. At the same time, she was also looking for her own cowboy, a macho mensch who knew how to fight and drive fast cars and who did not bullshit (המוח לא מזיין את),[24] someone who would take care of her and not the other way around.[25] In other words, Gafi Amir was not only a cowboy but also a damsel, distressed by the vagaries of dating and the frustrating search for the right man, or "soul mate," as Hollywood films taught us to call it. Both of these postures, the cowboy and the damsel, highlight Amir's naïve romanticism, her surprising belief in traditional values. Here was an innovative and fearless newspaperwoman, who went around upsetting carts while all she really wanted was to be domesticated by some "strong man." Her rhetoric may have been styled in ultra-contemporary jargon, but the values it promoted were notably old-fashioned, very much like Keret and Linur for that matter.

The Hebrew Amir used in her journalistic writing as well as in her more literary work reflected trendy argots more substantially than other romantic writers. These were the cutesy and precious modes of speech of Israel's new yuppies, the young, new Israeli urban class that was featured in her columns and read them. Sometimes, Amir overuses their language, which renders her literature manneristic and ultimately dated. But often her finely tuned re-creation of the contrived way these men and women speak constitutes a subtle but acute critique of their antics: "I speak like a bimbo (פרחה) as a way to protest." [26]

Here is the opening to the first story, "Begil esrim tagi'a layareyach" (*By Age 21 You Will Reach the Moon*), in her best and most representative work, an anthology of short stories by the same name:

> A friend of mine from high school, Doron, just turned thirty.
> He is so depressed that he sits around all day and reads
> the Visa catalogue. I wanted to take him out to celebrate
> somewhere, but in the end I got stuck at work till six. There
> was a power outage and all the computers crashed. "Don't
> ask, what a mess," I apologize. Doron sounds very drunk
> when I call in the evening to tell him that I couldn't get away
> till now. "It's all right," he says, delighted, "come here then
> and let's watch the yuppies from my porch." Gingerly, I ask
> him what he's doing. "I am reading the Visa catalogue," he
> says, "come over, I want to show you something." "Okay,"
> I say, "It's going to take me ten minutes," and in the end
> it takes me much longer. We hug warmly before I give
> him his present: a big and spotty fur frog. "It's so great you
> came," he says. "This is so cool, it's like bringing someone a

cockroach for a present." But I show him how it ribbets when you squeeze it. "Listen, listen," I plead, "it's a real ribbet." "Great," Doron says. "I'll put it on the TV. Get over here, I wanted to show you something." (7)

The passage is crowded with signs of advancing capitalism and the influence of its insignia, the popular media: a vapid obsession with aging, high-tech, conspicuous consumption, and the urban environment it all takes place in. Doron's depression is nothing but the affected whining of a pampered baby. He bemoans the passage of time—thirty is not old age, not even in relative terms—because he is influenced by a youth-obsessed culture, whose popular media is saturated with images of attractive and dynamic young men and women. Doron is an old man only because the kind of life that seems to matter in many films, television shows, and most commercials today lasts about one decade, between the ages of eighteen and thirty. "Man, I'm as old as dirt," he says to Nurit, the narrator and his friend (זקן זה מה אני ב׳ונה,). "I have more CDs and twice as many magazines from when I was twenty, and that's about it. And I thought that by thirty I'd already have a stylish duplex and a hot wife who'd put out every night" (תביא לי כל לילה).

The distinction Doron makes between what he possessed at the age of twenty, what he possesses now, at the age of thirty, and what he would have liked to possess is bogus, of course. There is no qualitative difference between CDs and magazines and a condo. These are all material possessions that only differ in price, not in kind. Doron talks about his wife in the same possessive way. Naturally, she would be attractive, just as his condo would be stylish. She would also service him sexually on a regular basis as if she were an expensive and reliable gadget. All of this would sound obnoxious if Doron were not so pathetic. "I have to show you what I found," he says to Nurit and picks up the Visa catalogue. "Look at this Japanese foot massager . . . and this pocketknife with twenty blades. I have to have it. This catalogue," he marvels, "I've been reading it since four o'clock and it's unbelievable. Look at all the choices they have here." [27]

Inundated by a plethora of choices, Doron is actually arrested, unable to go on with his life. He seems like a perpetual twenty-something, stuck, as it were, in what Eva Illouz calls the "capitalist realism" of commercials and ads. "Unlike classical utopias," writes Illouz, "the romantic utopia of advertising does not offer a narrative of progress, but instead implodes different temporalities within the category of romantic intensities." [28]

Illouz speaks about the use of romance to advertise various products, most ubiquitously vacations and getaways in which beautiful couples are seen secluded serenely on empty and immaculate beaches. Part of her point is that such ads inculcate consumption for its own sake, irrespective of the need for it or the ability to afford it. But the implication for Doron's life is clear: he seems to literally live in an ongoing present perpetuated by a continuous stream of pseudo-choices provided by advertising, in this case a credit card catalogue. Each of these "choices," like the Japanese foot massager and the nifty pocketknife, offers a new excitement that disappears as quickly as it appeared, like fireworks that explode spectacularly and fizz out a moment later.

Initially, Nurit plays along with Doron. After all, she belongs to his milieu and subscribes to many of its vanities. But when Doron continues to "shop," and says to her, "I feel like [having/getting] a baby," meaning he would like to have a child just as if he were saying, I feel like having a pocketknife or a Japanese foot massager, Nurit becomes truly depressed. "Sure, I think to myself, a baby, and get really irritated when I think of all the dreams I had and how they all ended in the garbage." Like Doron, she too envisioned a future life whose progression would be marked by the amassing of goods. She was going to be a supermodel, she was going to strut her stuff with a hunk slung over her arm; she was going to lose weight, win a Nobel, get very rich, and have someone write a poem about her. None of these are actual achievements but rather status symbols, a checklist borrowed from an instant culture that is more concerned with appearance than substance.

Nurit knows it. She is not as clueless or mercenary as she appears. "God," she thinks to herself as Doron describes how he would play with his baby after he came home from work. "If we talk about this even a second longer I'd really begin to feel sad." In fact, she is as sappy and as romantic as can be. She sighs and thinks about how "a spring evening wreaks havoc on my serotonin," how it gives her hope, and how it makes her think about the last man she loved. "Maybe something really good will happen to us this summer," she says to Doron, who takes her hand in his and promises: "Nurit, by the time you're twenty-one, you'll reach the moon." They both laugh, remembering how they cited these fortune cookie or Bazooka chewing gum clichés to one another years earlier when they still dated. "And one day," Nurit continues the nostalgic game, "you'll make an important scientific discovery." But when Doron becomes serious and earnestly asks her what she wishes for most, she does not hesitate to ask for her old boyfriend, Uri, to come back to her and tell her he cannot live without her. Her answer lifts the protective veil of cynicism she has wrapped around her, even though she tries to anxiously keep it in place by quickly changing the painful subject. "Look," she calls Doron's attention, "Yuppies . . ."

> From where we sit on the porch we can see the Shenkinites (שינקינאים) emerging out of their duplexes on their way to the cafés. . . . I'm sure their heads are abuzz with a name for the next new snack. Their creative thoughts rattle and bump against each other making a racket in the street. And that's good, because if they ever stopped and there'd be silence, I'll probably hear myself plead [to my old boyfriend], come back to me, please. (10)

But her attempt fails when Doron drops his cynical affectation and confesses that he too wants "love, Nurit, you understand, love."

Amir plays a double game here. The denigration of the Yuppies does not comfort the spurned lovers in the story. Not because there is anything wrong in badmouthing Yuppies, but because she knows that they play a symbolic social role. On the one hand Amir props them up and puts them on a pedestal while on the other hand she mocks them for that very role. Doron and Nurit buy into a system that promises to reward its members by elevating them to Yuppiedom. They openly crave that status and would like very much to join the upwardly mobile middle class. The entire evening is built around this group, watching it, talking about it, simulating its pastime by looking through the Visa catalogue and fantasizing about ordering from it. But their co-option also makes them miserable because it stands in they way of a much greater fulfillment, the pursuit of True Love. Both see this at the end and openly admit it although they do little to resist it. Nurit's frustration and pain come from her awareness, suppressed as it is, of this paradox. But her understanding of herself also holds the promise of a cure, a way out of a predicament over which she has a measure of control.

Ilanit, the heroine of a story called "Bayit katan ba'arava" (Little House in the Prairie), is sadder because she is oblivious to her manipulation by some of the same commercial forces, especially by what Illouz calls the media's obsessive representation of the romantic experience and its influence on our lives.[29] Ilanit is a working-class high school girl, whose drab life in a drab town, Bat-Yam, is mediated almost completely by the virtual reality of trashy television shows, soap operas or telenovelas, as they are known in Israel by their Spanish name. She is depressed because her boyfriend left her after she told him her period was late. Her mother is an unworldly housewife; her father is employed by the army as a janitor of sorts (רס״ר). None of them is especially equipped to deal with her complicated predicament, Ilanit thinks. "Why is it that on TV," she muses bitterly,

> on Beverly Hills [90210],[30] the mother always comes with a glass of orange juice for her daughter and a cup of coffee for herself and says: "Do you want to talk about it, honey?"[31]
> And then her daughter, with her honey-blond pigtails, goes: "I don't know what to do. My boyfriend kissed me yesterday evening and he told me he loves me." And let's say the mother hugs her, leans over her head and says: "You don't have to be ashamed it's natural," etc. etc.
> And only my mom is primitive. (121)

Ilanit's negative comparison of her dreary life to the glamorous life shown on TV is initially confirmed by the opening of the story, in which her "large, ungainly" mother shops for cosmetics. She cuts the line, shoves other customers, brusquely rummages through boxes of products on sale, and carries around a bag of groceries, including a frozen chicken that drips on the floor. When she sees her daughter crying she thinks it is because she did not get her the exact beauty product she asked for, so she promises to take her shopping for clothes instead. But when that does not work either, the mother begins to be annoyed. "What's the matter with you, Ilanit, are you out of your mind or something? Let's buy some cucumbers and go back home. I've had enough of you for one day." This is not at all like Jennet's mother from *The Sword of Love*, a pulp romance one of Ilanit's girlfriends in school reads and whose wisdom she shares with her. "Everything is going to be all right," says Jennet's mother, "you're my daughter and I'll do the best I can for your happiness." As Ilanit listens to her friend, she draws circles in the sand, just "like the heroine from *Mystery Woman* on cable TV." At one point Ilanit even fantasizes about carrying her pregnancy to its termination and having a child, "who'll be blond with blue eyes, and I'll dress him like Crystal's baby, and stroll with him in Tel-Aviv."[32] No wonder, then, that the ugliness of real life inconveniences Ilanit and upsets her.

The pathos of Ilanit's predicament needs little elaboration. She is completely imprisoned by that pervasive mythology of contemporary life, especially American life—romantic love (most of the shows she watches are made in the United States).[33] So much so, in fact, that she cannot see how much her mother really loves her, how much she cares for her, and how attuned she is to her needs. She cannot see it because it is right in front of her as part of her everyday life and because it does not unfold in the stylized way she is accustomed to seeing on television. Her mother may be vulgar, clumsy, and ugly, but she nevertheless freezes with fright when Ilanit haltingly tries to unburden her secret. "Mom's thick shoulders are lifted. Her back is wide in the floral pattern dress. . . . She puts her two red hands on the wet work surface. Ilanit, she says with horror, what's the matter with you, tell me." In her own simple way the mother is very tender and understanding. "She tells dad that I have a cyst that needs to be taken out in the hospital under local anesthesia and he doesn't ask anything more." Before the procedure, she insists on buying her a tuna sandwich from a hospital vending machine, even though she is not hungry. "Never mind, you'll eat it later, you'll be hungry. You haven't eaten anything today."

The tragedy of Ilanit's life is that no matter how unprivileged it is she continues to live in a virtual universe, a television fairyland governed by impossible scripts. Not even the trauma of having to go through a teen-age abortion shakes her back into reality. As she walks back into school at the end of the story, she thinks how "we don't have personal lockers here like in [the high school television show] *Degrassi*. . . . It kills me to think that there are people who are twenty times prettier, smarter, nicer, and more charming than me who greet each other affectionately and wish each other 'a nice day'" (129). For Ilanit, these fictional characters are real people whose "lives" mean much more to her than the demeaning "unreality" of her own life.

Gafi Amir "did not invent the Israeli female anti-hero," wrote Ariena Melamed, "but her minute accounts of that anti-heroine's squandered life, devoid of any hope for future happiness, are expressed with remarkable sharpness and accuracy."[34] These are not cynical accounts, however—on the contrary. Like her other literary peers, Amir focuses on the central idiom of the age—romance, both as a problem and a solution. Ilanit's great thirst for love in her life, her almost deliberately self-delusional pursuit of it, is very sad. But as this thirst for love repeats itself and accumulates in story after story, it is finally transformed and becomes a desperate but eloquent yearning for love, "for something that will fill the void of a miserable present with a new life and make the way for a more promising future."[35]

There is nothing new or special about the fact that Gadi Taub, Uzi Weil, and Gafi Amir base their works on their own lives and incorporate elements from their biographies into it. All authors do so. Dating, sex, love, and romance figure prominently in their works because most of these were written and published when they were in their twenties and naturally reflect what was uppermost in their minds at that time. The fact that all four stopped publishing sometime during their thirties, shortly before or after the second Intifada in 2000, has no doubt to do with personal reasons as much as with the changing political landscape. But the relatively short time frame of their literary activity and its limited scope contributed to their identity as a group and intensified their collective message. Besieged by the great changes that were all around them toward the end of the twentieth century, these writers attempted for a brief time to construct a different Israeli narrative, one that loosened the taut connections between the nation and its individual members. While their focus on romantic love may sometimes seem adolescent and immature, the wider resonance these writers had in the 1990s, and the immediate and fervid popularity they enjoyed then, amplified their personal belief in an inherently liberating and individualizing ideal. It also turned it into a grander mode of rebellion, escape, and fulfillment in an increasingly alienating world.

CONCLUSION

Whilst the romantic writers poignantly expressed the spirit of their age, ultimately, their literary flight—their attempt to lift off the bumpy Israeli surface and soar into the comfort of a smooth Western sky—was short-lived. The breaking of the second Intifada in 2000 with its devastating effects on the country resurrected the reality of a Middle East that does not allow, at least not yet, the manufacture of a new Israeli way of life through imported narratives. Certainly not when a very immediate reality was cruelly tearing those narratives apart and announcing itself ever more loudly each time a suicide bombing exploded in the country with increasing frequency toward the end of the 1990s. As the momentum of peace slowed after the assassination of Rabin in 1996, and the relations with the Palestinians cooled and soured, the Oslo Accords eventually expired as well. The country's euphoria of the decade's beginning gave way to a deep melancholia, exacerbated by the rising death toll of both soldiers and civilians. The borders around Israel seemed to close in tighter than ever before as the Hezbollah continued to bleed the army on the Lebanese front, and as suicide bombers added civilians to the mounting toll of deaths on the home front.

Literary history itself makes the 2000 dividing line visible. All of the romantic writers stopped publishing shortly before or after the second Intifada.[1] The reasons for it are numerous but surely they had something to do with the end of an era. The country's siege mentality, which returned toward the end of the millennium, was justified for once, even if Israel was largely responsible for it. The frequent attacks on buses, restaurants, and discos in the heart of the country were severely depressing, especially coming, as they did, on the heels of the earlier optimism. The heightened sense of personal danger fragmented the country deeper still, but it also aroused a sense of unity, a renewed form of tribalism that in some ways was more harmful than before. For those who believed in it, the steep fall from the grace of Oslo and the promise it held made reality all the more bitter and resulted in the dangerous unilateral moves Israel made in 2000 and 2005, the withdrawal of its troops from Lebanon and the evacuation of the Gaza Strip respectively. Both steps proved even in the short run to be detrimental to Israel, who found that it could not extricate itself out of an exasperating Middle East simply by walking away from Lebanon and building a fence between itself and the Palestinians.

From a literary perspective, the end of the era was marked by the fizzle of Keret, Taub, Weil, and Amir, who stopped writing, at least for a while, around that time. At the same time, the resurrection of some of the country's old demons inspired a new generation of young authors to engage once again with the greater national story, which was somewhat abandoned during the 1990s. "Abandonment" is an exaggeration, of course. Although the four romantic writers were popular, there were numerous other contemporary writers who were more prominent, and just as popular if not more so, and who continued to engage these issues throughout this time. The long list includes some of Israel's veteran writers, like S. Yizhar, Aharon Megged, and Yoram Kanuik, who had a second wind toward the end of the millennium; State Generation writers like Amos Oz, A. B. Yehoshua, Yehudit Hendel, Aharon Appelfeld, Yehoshua Kenaz, and Sami Michael, who continued to enrich the culture with their works; and later arrivers like David Grossman, Orly Castel-Bloom, and Ronit Matalon, to name but a few.

However—and this is where the literary historian walks on thin ice—most if not all of these writers began writing before the Intifada and as a matter of course continued the literary traditions of their predecessors. That is, they fulfilled the more traditional literary role of "prophet," as Shaked calls it (צופה לבית ישראל), and which Keret, Taub, Weil, and Amir relaxed or abandoned. By "prophesying" I mean creating a literature that was deeply and directly involved in the affairs of the nation, giving it perspective, illuminating it, admonishing it, analyzing it, and foreshadowing its future. Each of the novelists listed in the former paragraph engaged with one or more of these aspects, continuing a long tradition. The romantic writers were different in this respect. It is not that they quit the role of prophet completely. After all, this study is predicated on their message. But a great part of that message concerned disengagement, an attempt to look away and a refusal to participate in the (national) conversation. In the context of Hebrew literary tradition, the very attempt to do so was instructive and important.

Eventually, however, the changing times brought an end to this literary détente, which could not persist during a state of national emergency. Those writers who always stayed engaged and continued to "prophesy" throughout the 1990s cannot be used to mark the changes wrought by the second Intifada because the event did not have a discernible effect on their writing. They wrote after it as they did before. This is why young writers, who published their first works shortly after the second intifada, can signify the change more clearly: writers like Dudu Busi, Amir Gutfreund, Eshkol Nevo, and Ron Leshem. All of these neophyte writers published novels rather than short stories. The change in genre is significant. The short stories of the romantic writers, casual, hip, slangy, and young, expressed the frenzy and instability of their age, the plethora of its confusing choices, and the influence of the commercial media. The novels of Busi, Gutfreund, Nevo, and Leshem, return to a more measured perspective, one tempered by the sobering times and more directly informed by the Israeli literary tradition.[2]

As opposed to the romantic writers, each of these new novelists picks up an old, familiar theme and gives it new forms. Even more significantly, each of them also tries to suggest new paradigms of national unity that find expression in the compassionate tone and the traditional realism of their works. Dudu Busi's 2000 *Hayareyach yarok bavadi* (*The Moon Is Green in the Wadi*) is a post-Mizrahi bildungsroman that examines the genre afresh, dealing with Mizrahi issues without being mired in identity politics.[3] Amir Gutfreund's 2002 *Sho'a shelann* (*Our Holocaust*) embeds the memory of the Holocaust in the national gene pool beyond the second generation.[4] Eshkol Nevo's 2004 *Arba'a batim vega'agu'a* (*Osmosis*) literally romances the nation,[5] and Ron Leshem's 2005 *Im yesh gan eden* (*Beaufort*) reexamines the place of the IDF within Israeli society.[6]

Before I proceed with these new writers, I want to briefly return to a more veteran one, Orly Castel-Bloom, who marked the changes I just mentioned in illuminating ways. In Chapter 1 I noted the wild anarchy of Castel-Bloom's texts, the terror they raise, their profound sense of loss on the brink of a new era, and their inherent inability to make sense of an Israeli world that lost its anchoring in a grand national narrative. For all of these reasons, Castel-Bloom's first novel in the twenty-first century, the 2002 *Chalakim enoshiyim* (*Human Parts*), stands apart from her previous works with its (relative) realism in which a contemporary Israel under the relentless attacks of suicide bombers is decidedly recognizable.[7] I put "relatively" in parentheses because *Human Parts*, like Castel-Bloom's other works, still depicts a world that fundamentally does not make sense. But this time, the source of surrealism is more a product of the impossible political and social "situation," as Israelis call it, than it is Castel-Bloom's own literary construction. This is an important difference. Although the novel is fantastically set in an Israel beset by incessant rain and snow storms and sub-zero temperatures, the literal Ice Age is a metaphor for the political limbo of the country, and the perpetual cycle of violence. The bitter effects of the harsh winter draw attention to the impossibility of the political quagmire by aggravating its impact.

"It was an exceptional winter," begins the novel,

> in the mountains the temperature was almost always below zero. . . . Raindrops the size of olives fell in multitudes . . . hailstones were gigantic. . . . Owing to the heavy snow drifts, trees planted by the pioneers early in the previous century fell to the ground. . . . Yet as if the outlandish winter wasn't enough . . . the peace process with the Palestinians . . . collapsed like one of the houses whose roof gave way under the weight of the snow. (3–5)[8]

Israel in *Human Parts* is a merciless place plagued from the inside as from without. Its characters have little understanding and compassion for one another, not even in the face of the deadly fate that threatens them all. What separate them are not so much ethnic or political differences as much as wealth: widening gaps between the rich, who isolate themselves from the harsh winter in their plush apartments and luxurious cars, and the poor, who have no money for heating or warm clothes. Many of the commonalities that held them together before despite their differences seem to have disappeared. In this new and cruel Israeli universe of dog eat dog, the only uniting element is the Hebrew text. The obvious connection that binds the alienated characters is their common fate; the death by suicide bombing that threatens them at random, rich or poor.

This was a new development for Castel-Bloom.[9] A central feature of her previous works from the 1980s and 1990s, which earned her postmodern credentials, was her penchant for eliminating the logical connections between syntax and lexicon.[10] *Human Parts* reestablishes these linguistic connections. Only now, the described reality itself does not make sense: "The country was drenched with every form of precipitation. . . . Navy ships were anchored in places no one could have imagined possible before the onslaught. . . . Sailboats were seen in Petah-Tikva, in Or Yehuda, in Mazkeret Batya, in Kfar Saba . . ." (4). This is a logical description of an extremely bizarre situation. The surrealism is external, not linguistic and internal. If the country is flooded, it makes sense that ships would be seen in what were formerly dry, low-lying lands. The same surface or superficial tightness holds the novel's disparate characters together.[11] The wealthy siblings Adir and Liat Dubnov, Adir's former girlfriend, the impoverished divorcée Iris Ventura, his new girlfriend, the Ethiopian supermodel Tasaro, and the destitute Kati Bet-Halahmi and her husband, Boaz, have little in common save for the proximate lives they lead in an ever-shrinking Israel. But as the tight text makes very clear, there are still strong ties that bind these people together.

After more than a decade of writing strident prose about the dissolution and fragmentation of Israeli society, *Human Parts* presents for the first time in the works of Castel-Bloom a picture of a more cohesive Israel. This is not the picture of a strong and integrated society by any means. Rather it is a patched-up union comprised of different people and groups who are held together by fear and by a shared, dismal, fate that is accentuated by the Jewish time that frames the novel.[12] At the same time, the inclusion of the various groups that make up Jewish Israel—the founding, Ashkenazi elite of the country, working-class Mizrahim as well as recent Ethiopian and Russian immigrants—renders the novel more than a little symbolic, so that the close textual proximity of the characters and their collective destiny also has a comforting and, ultimately, perhaps even a redemptive message.[13]

Castel-Bloom's relative new realism received a much more traditional treatment by Busi, Gutfreund, Nevo, and Leshem, whose works are generically conservative by comparison. Take for example Dudu Busi's remarkably mature first novel, *The Moon Is Green in the Wadi*, a compelling coming-of-age story about a young man who grows up in the 1970s in Shkhunat Hatikvah, one of Tel-Aviv's most neglected Mizrahi neighborhoods. In some ways, the novel is part of a long tradition of similar bildungsroman that involve underprivileged Mizrahim who manage to escape their harsh environment against many odds: dysfunctional family, discouraging environment, and suspicious and alienating (Ashkenazi) establishment. The most immediate examples of similar works are the novels of Sami Michael and Eli Amir, who introduced the genre in the 1970s and 1980s. Busi's novel, however, lacks the apologetic tone that Michael and Amir sound at times; the attempt to showcase the richness of Mizrahi culture in the face of its Ashkenazi detractors. At the same time, *Moon* does not wrap itself up in a seclusive Mizrahi culture that rejects all forms of Ashkenazi Israeliness, which characterized Mizrahi cultural trends in the 1990s.[14] Instead, the novel is a direct and serious social engagement with economic and other difficulties.

The Mizrahi culture in the novel is neither excused nor eulogized. It is a natural part of the protagonist's, Mousa's, environment. Some parts of it, like his family, the intimacy of the community, the ethnic richness, and his place in it, are dear to him. Other parts, like the physical and mental decrepitude and the violence, are decidedly unattractive. But nowhere in the novel is there a sense of ethnic injustice, an accusation, veiled or direct, about ethnic oppression. In fact, *Moon* is much more conservative than that. It is one of those classic novels of adversity that end (relatively) happily with the hero overcoming (almost) all of the obstacles that stood in his way. But in the context of the genre in Israel this is precisely what makes the work new and unusual. *Moon* is different because it wages a socialist fight rather than an ethnic or identity fight. To the extent that the novel engages in ethnic politics, it subsumes it under a bigger social agenda as part of class struggle in Israel. The message of unity in the book is thus the erasure of the Mizrahi-Ashkenazi divide in favor of a more meaningful struggle for socio-economic parity.

Our Holocaust suggests similarly uniting aspects by examining the influence of the Holocaust on a younger generation of Israelis, who are "twice and a half" removed from it, as the author put it. The young protagonist is not of the first or second generation of Holocaust survivors, but farther removed from the mid-twentieth-century horrors. One of the most surprising aspects of the novel is the ways it copes with the catastrophe. Unlike Aharon Appelfeld, whose austere prose and spectral narratives have come to define Israeli Holocaust literature, Gutfreund writes a Holocaust story rich in detail, luxuriant in style, humorous, and even upbeat. The tragic diminution of the hero's family in the Holocaust occupies him, but since he is so removed from it, by time, by space, and even by culture, they fertilize his psyche more than haunt it. The Holocaust is less menacing to him than powerful and compelling.

When it came out, the novel was understandably compared to Grossman's *See Under: Love*, which also deals with the Holocaust through the eyes of a young child. But the similarities end with the mutual premise. Grossman's novel is about the inability to comprehend the Holocaust as a unique event. By trying to "crack" its secret in different ways, Grossman emphasizes again and again that the Holocaust is beyond grasp, beyond words, beyond sense. Gutfreund, on the other hand, attempts to do the opposite, to appropriate the Holocaust and give it definite, imaginable values. The "our" of the title refers to the young hero and his cousin, who make the Holocaust "their own" by imagining their dead relatives' stories and making those "memories" part of their games and eventually their Israeli lives as well. But the possessive pronoun also turns the Holocaust into an inclusive legacy of the nation and maybe even beyond. Through an engaging narrative that weaves horror, fantasy, and adventure, readers are invited to perceive the Holocaust not as something unimaginable that happened on "another planet," in the words of Ka-tzetnik, but as "ordinary events, perpetrated by ordinary people whose victims were ordinary people" as well, as Gutfreund phrased it.[15]

It may be argued that *Our Holocaust*, coming as it did in the wake of two Intifadas, fails to internalize the lessons of Jewish suffering, especially for a people as persecuted as the Jews. Engaging with the biggest tragedy that ever befell the Jews so close to the contemporary suffering of the Palestinians may seem selfish and insensitive in a way, maybe heartless, even if it were a mere publishing coincidence. On the other hand, the universalizing message of the novel, the fact that the "our" of the title makes the tragedy potentially every reader's, holds sobering lessons as well. If ordinary people could act so horribly toward other ordinary people, it means that such "ordinary" events can happen again anywhere and can be perpetrated by anyone, even in Israel and even by Jews. Whether this may be a bit of an interpretive stretch, the fact remains that *Our Holocaust* speaks once again about the common national past as well as about its transcendent legacy.

Although the third novel, *Osmosis*, is a love story, national politics, society, and culture play an important role in the romance. So much so, in fact, that the nation constitutes one of the novel's most important characters and functions like the extended family of the young couple at its center, whose own families are absent from the story. Like A. B. Yehoshua's *Hame'ahev* (*The Lover*) (1977), the story in *Osmosis* is conveyed from multiple perspectives through first-person narratives of various characters: the Ashkenazi Amir and his Ashkenazi girlfriend, No'a, their Mizrahi neighbor, Sima, an old Palestinian construction worker, Tsadek, and a young teenager, Yotam, who lost his brother in Lebanon.[16] The pervasive influence of national politics on the story should be clear from this list that could never be compiled about the works of any of the romantic writers. Politics seeps into the most intimate places and moments in *Osmosis*, shapes the story and directs it. The murder of Rabin and the depression that spreads in its wake affect the relations between Amir and No'a; the tension between secular and religious in

Israel almost rip Sima and her husband apart; after Yotam's brother dies in Lebanon his family decides to leave the country for good; and the Palestinians, represented by Tsadek, remain downtrodden and voiceless, a constant and unpleasant specter.

Little of the "selfish" romantic rights and privileges that lovers in stories by Keret, Taub, Weil, and Amir enjoy are left for Noʿa and Amir. Their love unfolds against a raw background of political turmoil, national violence, social tensions, ethnic discrimination, pain, loss, and death, which often interfere with their very lovemaking. The lovers themselves are symbolic entities. As a native of Jerusalem, Amir is more sombre and complex, like the city of his birth. As a native of Tel-Aviv, Noʿa is more lighthearted, communicative, and spontaneous. Unable to commit to either city permanently, the two settle temporarily in a small town between them. Indeed, the quest for a permanent "home" in the multiple meanings of the term is central to the novel, whose Hebrew title literally reads: Four Homes and a Yearning. Each of the voices in this collection of characters is yearning for a home, and although none of them finds it, their ensemble literary performance and their persistent longing are signs of hope.

The last work, Ron Leshem's *Beaufort,* is a gritty military action novel that follows closely an infantry combat unit in Lebanon on the eve of Israel's withdrawal from that country in 2000. Leshem based the novel on real events, although not on personal experience. In a postscript, he relates how he got the idea for the novel after meeting an exhausted and disappointed IDF officer, who served a few harrowing years facing the Hezbollah in southern Lebanon, and after the army's withdrawal from that country was reassigned to police the Gaza Strip. Leshem is a prominent journalist and his novel is one of the first serious works that deals with Israel's eighteen-year stay in Lebanon (1982–2000). The aftermath of Israel's first war in Lebanon and the media's engagement with it are interrelated in the novel as a comment on the changing perception and role of the IDF in Israeli society.

The back cover of the novel tells readers that *Beaufort* "echoes the voice of a generation of soldiers who fought in the name of camaraderie (רעות) and dreamt about distant shores." Camaraderie in this context refers to the mythological friendships that Israel's many wars fostered between its fighting men, forging them into a band of brothers. The distant shores refer to the extended post-army trips many young Israelis take to the Far East, in order to distance and disconnect themselves for a while from the pressure cooker at home. The dissonance between the two has to do with the genesis of Israeli military camaraderie, which originated in the 1948 War of Independence and was mythologized in poetry, prose, and popular culture. The power of the myth came from the prize that the fighting men, dead or alive, were awarded—an independent state. Ironically, Leshem's soldiers dream of something very different—the distant shores of India and Thailand.

The novel strikingly records a paradigmatic shift that reflects many of the changes that the romantic writers sensed as well. The soldiers' extraordinary courage in *Beaufort* is not motivated by selfless patriotism as much as by their devotion to their comrades and a "selfish" desire to excel. They view their ability to survive in the deadly war zone as a form of extreme sport.[17] This may not take away from their worth as soldiers nor from the worthiness of their service. But it does point to a dangerous gap that opened up shortly after the first Lebanon war between the army and the Israeli people in the name of whom it serves. As the media continued to criticize the government's Lebanon policy by lambasting the army that carried it out, soldiers like the ones depicted in *Beaufort* found themselves increasingly conflicted and alienated from the civilian population they served and protected.[18] Volunteering for service in what they initially thought was a just cause, they eventually found the value of that cause disputed and devalued. The "uniting" message of Leshem, then, is to draw attention to the dangers of this split and warn that a small and beleaguered country like Israel whose army is truly civilian cannot afford to send its soldiers to fight in the name of causes that are deeply controversial.

I mentioned these four novels because their direct re-engagement with some of the nation's most pressing issues, and especially their thirst for a national consensus of some kind, stand in clear contrast to the focus of the romantic writers. It is too early to know whether the shift marks the beginning of a new stage or a cultural age in Israel. But as the second war in Lebanon in 2006 demonstrated, the time for a postzionist or a postnational age has not yet come. If Israel's first war in the twenty-first century has made one thing clear, it is that the wholesale privatization that began in the mid-1980s has failed—not just that of the economy, but especially the kind of privatization of society and culture that *Ha'ir* promoted. This is not an indictment. *Ha'ir* was one agent in a greater cultural revolution that may have pushed the free-market pendulum too much in one direction, including the free market of ideas. Some of the problems this has caused were demonstrated almost symbolically during the war of 2006 by the shower of rockets that rained on the north of Israel. Notwithstanding the inability of the IDF—itself a casualty of privatization—to stop the rain of bombs, the absence of a State "umbrella" that could adequately care for the besieged citizens of the north, especially the poor, the old, and the infirm, exposed the consequences of post-nationalism.

Despite the controversy about who won that war, Hezbollah or Israel, the issue is not military at all. "Why don't we let Gaidamak buy out the army and be done with it," said one soldier who returned from Lebanon in the summer of 2006.[19] "This way," he continued, "we'll be sure to receive brand new weapons, excellent gear, and a nice logo on our uniform. Maybe he'll even make a deal with Hezbollah and pay them not to attack us." Arkadi Gaidamak was a wealthy businessman and philanthropist who was the first to respond to some of the civil havoc wreaked by the war. About a week after it began he set up a well-stocked tent city in the south of Israel to shelter Israelis who fled the north.[20] Three weeks later, too little and too late, the government responded by setting up similar shelters. Commenting at the end of an inconclusive ground campaign that appeared to have been waged in hesitation and conducted with indecision, the soldier may have spoken glibly, but perspicaciously nevertheless. "With bitter irony," wrote Avirama Golan, "that young man defined the mood of the society in which he grew up and of which he became a citizen; a society that succumbed to a duplicitous discourse that touted privatization and promised a magic wand that would quickly resolve the [Arab-Israeli] conflict and bring about peace, or that would at least entertain us while we waited for it."

Golan does not argue with the desire to have a normal, comfortable, or even pampered life. The war has actually proven the endurance of many of *Ha'ir*'s civic values, mainly in the ways the public in Israel reacted to the incompetent management of the war. The unprecedented media coverage of the war exposed the political and military decision-making process to the scrutiny of an alert and educated public that was rightly upset by the ineptitude of its leaders. Much of the criticism after the war was leveled at the cavalier way in which the government went to war, the way it neglected its soldiers and abandoned its citizens in the north. "Not Sparta and a Good Thing Too," read one article, which understood the military defeat as a victory for the country's civic character.[21] The fact that Israelis worry about the lives of soldiers, and the loss of life's comforts and pleasures, argued the pundit, does not mean that they are effete or weak; on the contrary. It speaks to the country's wish to remain a comfortable, civil, and democratic society and not a Masada-like fortress.[22]

Golan does think, however, that neither the unity and purpose needed to maintain a fortress, nor the robust legal, economic, and cultural foundations needed for the maintenance of a healthy democratic society, can survive without a solid social contract. The continued erosion of that civil contract, she writes, was glaringly exposed during the 2006 war by the government's neglect of the country's northern region. When the worship of mammon accompanies extreme individualism, warns Golan, it can create acute social alienation that becomes detrimental to the health of society as well as to its ability to make peace with its neighbors. If the Israeli poor are fed a steady diet of anti-Arab jingoism instead of real solutions to their socio-economic concerns, neither peace nor economic parity will ensue, concludes Golan.

It would be unfair and inaccurate to say that the romantic writers were not interested in those issues at all. They were. Very much so. But their engagement took a different form and they often dealt with some of the exterior signs of the changing times, like popular culture, language, and visual imagery. Attuned to contemporary trends, they commented on substance through an engagement with surface or style. They were often misunderstood because of it. Pundits like Gideon Sammet, for instance, called them "stutterers," "manneristic," and "navel-gazers," and accused them of missing an opportunity to effect change in a meaningful way.[23] But perhaps the missed opportunity was his, an opportunity to read those texts as a direct and maybe even the only possible engagement with very confusing times.

The second Intifada and especially the second war in Lebanon rewound Israel to an earlier era and resurrected once again some of the existential fears that haunted it before Oslo. As a result, the postmodernist engagement with the old-new reality appeared hollow, ineffectual, or inconsequential indeed, as reality found a painful way to escape its manipulated representation. But by that time, the entire culture seemed infected with it. And while postmodernism can be intriguing when applied to art, it can be quite harmful when it determines politics. "The fault line (שֶׁבֶר) that was revealed in the war," wrote Uzi Benziman, "reflects the ills of society at large; a society that trifles with appearances instead of engaging with essentials (עטיפות לעומת מהות), and succumbs to a decision-making process by professionals bent on making impressions rather than effecting real change."[24] So while the war in Lebanon demonstrated the limits of cultural innovation and the construction of an imagined, Western Israel, it also resurrected the thirst for new national symbols and for a uniting paradigm around which to rally.

NOTES

INTRODUCTION

1. The first Zionist Congress, announcing the intention to establish a Jewish state in Palestine, was held in 1897. The State of Israel was established fifty-one years later, in 1948.

2. Gershon Shaked was the most persuasive proponent of this distinguishing feature. His generic division is largely predicated on it in his five-volume historiography, *Hebrew Fiction 1880–1980* (Keter, Hakibbutz Hameuchad, 1980).

3. See my review of his five-volume work in *Prooftexts*, Vol. 23, No. 3, Fall 2003.

4. See Alan Mintz, ed., *The Boom in Israeli Literature* (Hanover, N.H.: University Press of New England, Brandeis University Press, 1997); Avner Holtzman, *Mapat Drachim* (Hakibbutz Hameuchad, 2005).

5. See Abraham Balaban, *Gal Aher Basifrut Ha'ivrit: siporet ivrit postmodernistit* (Jerusalem: Keter, 1995). For a list of specific articles from the period, see below.

6. On the history and complexity of sex and love in Western culture, see Peter Gay's illuminating study, *Education of the Senses, The Bourgeois Experience: Victoria to Freud*, Volume I (New York: W. W. Norton & Company, 1984).

7. Although I usually label these writers "romantic," I sometimes use "First Person Dual" instead in order to emphasize different aspects of their writing.

8. See Robert Polhemus, *Erotic Faith* (Chicago and London: University of Chicago Press, 1990), in which he documents and investigates the connections between romance and the novel during the genre's heyday in the nineteenth century.

9. Eva Illouz, *Consuming the Romantic Utopia: Love and the Cultural Contradictions of Capitalism* (Berkeley: University of California Press, 1997).

10. A spiritual quest is also an important impetus for these trips, especially to India. See Elhanan Near, ed., *Mehodu ve'ad kan: hogim yisre'elim kotvim al hodu vehayahadut shelahem* (Tel-Aviv: Me'ah She'arim, 2006), in which Israeli thinkers write about the influence of India on their Jewish spirituality.

11. While the economy continued to flourish in the 2000s after a short slump, it benefited an ever decreasing number of people. The earlier hopes of spreading the wealth more evenly and expanding the middle class were dashed as the Israeli economy became more harshly capitalistic. The gaps between rich and poor grew while at the same time the state abandoned many of its former social services.

12. This book focuses on Israeli culture. But the changes it examines are part of much larger, global trends. What the contemporary cultural critic Slavoj Žižek describes as "the end-of-ideology politics"—which characterize the late capitalist or global age—marked other national cultures and literatures during the same time (see Slavoj Žižek, *The Universal Exception* [London, New York: Continuum, 2007], 206). Žižek talks about the usurpation of politics by economics, the degeneration of a genuine political process that occurs when capital is no longer generated by and associated with national economies but instead serves the interests of supra-national, global conglomerates which are motivated by profit only, irrespective of other concerns.

The very fall of Russian communism toward the end of the millennium is a case in point: the collapse of an intensely ideological movement that gave way to a capitalist oligarchy that did away with real democratic politics altogether. On a smaller scale, Polish literature after the fall of communism can serve as another example that is closer to the Israeli case. The relaxing of ideological constraints in Poland and the rather violent change to a capitalist economy saw the emergence of a multitude of literary voices, among them young writers who focused on the personal as a repudiation of party cultural politics and a reaction to the confusion of the times. Postmodernism played a brief but significant part in Polish literature as well, although by 2000 it all but disappeared and Polish writers began to abandon their preoccupation with the private and personal and returned to examine broader themes of more national import; see Robert Osta-shevsky, "Haproza Hapolanit bashanim 1989–2000" (Polish Prose 1989–2000), *Mit'an*, Vol. 12 (Fall 2007): 27–29.

CHAPTER 1

1. Gadi Taub, *Hamered Hashafuf* (Tel-Aviv: Hakibbutz Hameuchad, 1997).

2. On the significance of the Six-Day War in Israeli history and its profound influence on its culture and politics, see Tom Segev, *1967* (Tel-Aviv: Hakibbutz Hameuchad, 2005).

3. I am referring here to the 1970s and 1980s, during which Israel's military and economic power were firmly established and were not yet eroded morally by the escalating conflict with the Palestinians and its current reverberations in Israeli and world politics.

4. Taub, *Hamered Hashafuf*, 13–14.

5. Meir Shalev, *Blue Mountain* (Edinburgh: Canongate, 2001). David Grossman, *See Under: Love* (New York: Farrar Straus Giroux, 1989), and *The Book of Intimate Grammar* (New York: Farrar Straus Giroux, 1994). Orly Castel-Bloom, *Doli Siti* (Tel-Aviv: Zmora-Bitan, 1992). Yosef Al-Dror, *The Obvious* (Tel-Aviv: Yediot Aharonot—Sifre Hemed, 1998).

6. In a provocative article that attracted a flurry of heated responses, literary critic Dan Miron, one of the pillars of the Israeli academy, wrote about this very shift. Titled: "This Generation Is Lost" (*Hador haze Avud*), the 1994 article laments an end of an era. "Thirty years after declaring the death of the 1948 Generation in Hebrew literature," begins the article, "professor Dan Miron announces that the writers of the 'New Wave' have also reached the end of their road. Amos Oz is in a state of major decline, Meir Shalev is a marginal phenomenon, David Grossman is increasingly diminishing, and A. B. Yehoshua just wrote a bad novel (*Hashiva mehodu* or *Open Heart*, Y. P.). These writers, says Miron, are self-centered and self-pitying," *Musaf Ha'aretz*, August 7, 1994, 18–20. One of Miron's major complaints is precisely that the works of these major writers do not deal anymore with the kind of central, national issues that were the bread and butter of modern Hebrew literature from its inception. The article reverberated in the national press for almost six months, attracting responses and counter-responses in the tradition of the great literary-cultural debates that had flared up periodically in the Hebrew press since the nineteenth century. That it was one of the last debates of its kind is in itself significant of the changing times and the democratization and decentralization of Hebrew-Israeli culture.

7. For a partial list of the many articles and studies that were dedicated to the novel, see the online catalogue of the Lexicon of Modern Hebrew Literature at: http://library.osu.edu/sites/users/galron.1/00070.php.

8. Shalev, *Blue Mountain*, 1.

9. *Lo rachok mimerkaz ha'ir* (Tel-Aviv: Am Oved, 1987). A representative sample from the frequent references to *Not Far from the City Center* in the daily press during 1987 reads: "Castel-Bloom manages to conjure up, through spare linguistic devices, a blank microcosm in which terrible things take place under the cloak of negligence and apathy" (Neta Ne'eman, "Bikoret," *Ma'ariv*, July 27, 1987). In 1990, David Gurevitz already labels Castel-Bloom as one of Israel's premier postmodernist writers in a detailed article titled "What Language Shall We Speak Tomorrow" (Be'ezo safa nedaber mahar), *Yediot Aharonot*, February 20, 1990.

10. Dan Miron, "Something about Orly Castel-Bloom" (Mashehu al Orly Castel-Bloom), *Al Hamishmar*, August 16, 1989.

11. Ariel Hirshfeld, "Castel-Bloom in Wonderland" (Castel-Bloom be'eretz hapla'ot), *Ha'aretz*, May 18, 1990.

12. Ortzion Bartana, "Where Are We" (Hechan anachnu nimtza'im), *Moznayim*, June–July 1992.

13. Ibid., 30. Bartana identifies precisely the postmodernist aspects in Castel-Bloom's works but is skeptical of their efficacy as literary devices. In his opinion, the hyper-realism of postmodernism undermines the text's ability to redeem.

14. Amnon Jacont, "Bad Aura" (Hilla ra'ah), *Yediot Aharonot*, February 8, 1989.

15. Gurevitz, "What Language Shall We Speak Tomorrow."

16. Unsigned, *Ha'aretz*, July 3, 1987.

17. Ariana Melamed, "Hallucinations from the Depth of Oppression" (*Hazayot mima'amakey hadikuy*), *Ha'ir*, June 9, 1996.

18. Orly Toren, "Love Is a Depth Charge inside the Soul" (*Ahava ze ptzatzat omek betoh haneshama*), *Yerushalayim*, January 6, 1989.

19. See Avner Bernheimer in *Ma'ariv*, December 30, 1994; David Gurevitz, "Recycled Dreams" (*Halomot memuhzarim*), *Iton 77*, March 1996, 38–43; and Abraham Balaban, *Gal Aher Basiporet Ha'ivrit: siporet ivrit postmodernistit* (Jerusalem: Keter, 1995). I discuss the media revolution in the next chapter.

20. For more on this, see the next chapter.

21. Interview with Nili Landesman, "Noshchim et halashon," *Ha'ir*, November 1, 1996, 54.

22. The show featured some of the cultural leaders of young Israel then, including Shalom Rosenfeld, Dan Ben-Amotz, Haim Hefer, Dan Almagor, and others. See Oz Almog, *Predah mi-srulik: shinui arachim ba-elitah ha-yisre'elit* (Haifa University, Zmora-Bitan Publishing, 2004), 1:96.

23. The trio's phenomenal success for three decades, from the 1960s through the 1980s, was predicated among other things on the tension created by the Jewish-ethnic differences that separates their stage personas.

24. Interview with Ayelet Shachar, "Ben harada lekapriza," *Ha'ir*, August 6, 1993, 50. Taub uses this quote as a motto for one of the chapters in his book.

25. Ibid.

26. Levin's intense satires were much more popular during the 1970s and 1980s than during the 1990s. Their intense ideological critiques of the establishment lost some of their poignancy in the more morally vague era between the two Intifadas. The renewed interest in Levin's satirical cabaret in 2004 may be another indication of the end of Al-Dror's era. See Tsipi Shohat, "A Popular Revival to 'You, Me and the Next War'" (*Hatzlacha lechidush "ani ve'at vehamilchama haba'a"*), *Ha'aretz*, November 8, 2004.

27. *Back Cover*, August 6, 1988. The quote is a paraphrase of Gertrude Stein.

28. Yosef Al-Dror, *The Obvious* (*Hamuvan me'elav*) (Tel-Aviv: Yediot Aharonot\Sifre Hemed, 1998).

29. Nili Landesman, "Noshchim et halashon."

30. An obvious example would be terminology that replaces negatively perceived labels like "retarded" with new and more neutral terms like "mentally handicapped" or "challenged"; "dwarf" with "little person"; or the more comical

inventions that were coined as a backlash to political correctness, such as "vertically challenged" for short, etc. Al-Dror often plays with these conventions and rails against them.

31. Al-Dror, *The Obvious*, 117–118.

32. I am referring here both to social and civil welfare at home, like the distribution of wealth and civil rights to women, blacks, and immigrants in the United States or to Muslims and immigrants in Europe, for instance, and to the self-interest of the same countries in their foreign affairs; interfering in the affairs of some countries (most recently Iraq) while neglecting others (like Rwanda).

33. This is true even of the revolutionary personalization of history in the Hebrew Bible, as Erich Auerbach shows in his well-known study of it, *Mimesis*. Although the symbolic significance of Abraham, for instance, is derived from his alleged existence as a historical figure, it ultimately transcends it, especially for a community of believers.

34. The erosion began many years before, after the establishment of the State in 1948. But its final collapse came in the late 1980s and 1990s; hence the sense of ideological vacuum Al-Dror speaks of. See Ze'ev Sternhall's discussion of the Zionist pioneering ethos. Sternhall credits the success of the State's founders to their single-mindedness, but he also faults them for it. "The old political elite did not realize the extent of the revolution which the State's establishment and the mass immigration required. Most of all, it did not understand the dire need to accommodate the rights of individuals. . . . The only rights the founders and their offspring recognized were Jewish historical rights. . . . In the last analysis, it is highly doubtful if this legacy can provide sufficient fuel for the future." "To Admire or Forget?" (*Leha'aritz o lishkoach—ma notar meha'aliya hashniya*), *Ha'aretz*, January 6, 2005.

35. Shachar, "Ben harada lekapriza."

36. Landesman, "Noshchim et halashon," 56.

37. Ibid.

CHAPTER 2

1. Haifa University Press/Zmora-Bitan.

2. Ibid., 142.

3. Ibid.

4. See for example the retrospective volume of one of Israel's most prolific early photographers, Rudi Weisenstein, who recorded many such scenes, in *Tzalmania*, ed. Daniela Di-Nur (Am Oved, no year).

5. The most recent representation of this imagery could be seen on the cover of the *Time Out Tel-Aviv* of August 2006, during the war with Hezbollah that summer. The cover carried an illustrated map of Israel divided by the Yarkon river north of Tel-Aviv. While to the north of the river bombs were falling

and people huddled in shelters, south of the river people lounged on the beach and in cafés.

Another article from that war, "Why Does Tel-Aviv Annoy Them," by Avirama Golan, discusses the alleged Tel-Aviv detachment and its indulgent "life goes on" attitude during the war. Golan refutes the premise for much the same reasons I mention above. "Lama Tel-Aviv me'atzbenet otam," *Ha'aretz*, August 23, 2006.

6. During the only time so far in the history of Israel that Tel-Aviv was under serious attack—in the 1991 Gulf War—many of the city's residents simply left the city for safer quarters. Rather than live an abnormal life in their normal city, they chose instead to leave it altogether. They were briefly scolded for it by their then mayor, Cheech, who was promptly derided for his parochialism by many of the city's residents. The period is parodied cleverly in Irit Linur's novel *Siren Song*, which is discussed in Chapter 3.

7. Almog, *Predah mi srulik*, 143.

8. Ibid., 147.

9. Doron Rosenblum, "The Expanding Jurisdiction of the Local Weekly" (*Tchum hashiput haholech umitrahev shel hamekomon*), *Ha'ir*, April 27, 1990. The article was a reprint from the fifth anniversary of *Ha'ir* in 1985.

10. Ibid.

11. See his chapter about the revolution in the written press. Almog, *Predah mi srulik*, 117–174.

12. The anthology was published under the same title (Tel-Aviv: Am Oved, 1994).

13. Tel-Aviv: Dvir, 1999. The stories, which were first published collectively in 1959, depict life in Tel-Aviv during the 1910s and 1920s.

14. Jewish and non-Jewish visitors to the city during its early days were repeatedly impressed with this clean and orderly outpost of the West in the East. For one representative example of these impressions, see David Frishman's travel notes from his 1911 visit to Palestine, "Hayadata et ha'arets? Reshimot masa be'eretz yisrael," *Hatzfira*, May 22, 1911, 1.

15. See Ya'acov Shavit and Gideon Bieger, *Hahistoria shel Tel-Aviv* (*The History of Tel-Aviv*) (Tel-Aviv: University of Tel-Aviv Press, 2001), 19.

16. *Yedidenu hakaspomat* (Our Friend the ATM), February 4, 1986.

17. Gutman, *Ir ktana*, 15.

18. The Hebrew word for "course" used here, חוג, denotes educational activities like after-school sports and enrichment programs for children, book clubs, bridge clubs, lectures, and other such activities for adults. A few years later Mohar wrote another amusing article in that vein, this time about the arrival of sadomasochism in Tel-Aviv; see "In the Age of Sado-Maso" (*Be'idan hasado-mazo*), July 22, 1994, 40.

19. See for example posters disseminated by the Jewish National Fund (JNF) for its campaign to develop the Negev in the south of Israel during the 1950s. "Let

the Vision of the Negev Stand: Redemption and Water to the Plains of the Wilderness" (יקום חזון הנגב—גאולה ומים לערבות השממה), reads one of many JNF posters from that time. The poster depicts red-roofed houses and green trees like an oasis in the midst of a yellow desert. From a postcard of an exhibition of Zionist propaganda posters at the Farkash Gallery in Tel-Aviv. The artist is Frantz Kraus.

20. The quote was used very frequently. For examples see an exhibition catalogue, *Kachol lavan bitzva'im: dimuyim chazutiyim shel hatziyonut, 1897–1947* (*Blue and White in Colors: Visual Representations of Zionism, 1897–1947*) (Diaspora Museum/Am-Oved, 1996).

21. The jingoistic socialism of Israel's labor party always had detractors, some of whom were brazen and loud, like Uri Avneri in his paper *Ha'olam Hazeh*, but their appeal was always limited. *Ha'ir* changed that.

22. The chapter was based on an article by the same name he wrote for *Ha'ir*, "Hadiktatura shel hapoza," January 20, 1995.

23. Taub, *Hamered hashafuf*, 37.

24. Gal Uchovsky, "Chad Gadia," *Tarbut Ma'ariv*, April 5, 1997, 14–15.

25. *Ha'ir*, June 12, 1986, 27.

26. "Haya eser, rishmei nesi'ah be'otobus komotayim baderech Liyerushalayim," June 29, 1990, 32.

27. Taken from "Extra Curricular Courses in Giv'atayim," noted above.

28. Another indication of the sexual revolutionary agenda of *Ha'ir* was the brief column "Letters from Zohar" (*Michtavim mizohar*), which listed the casual sexual adventures of its female writer. On August 5, 1994, p. 113, Zohar writes about a one-night stand she had with a cute, hitchhiking soldier she picked up in her car. She subsequently remembers that she actually knows him, she was his babysitter a long time ago. The idea behind the column was to provide an outlet for alternative female sexuality, more aggressive and predatory.

29. Two papers carried limited gay sections, *Ha'ir* in 1986–1987 and *Davar* from 1991 until it closed in 1996. There were three other attempts to publish gay papers, all of them abortive. For a concise history of gay media in Israel, see Orna Kazin, "No Liftoff" (*Ze lo mitromem*), *Ha'ir*, March 10, 1995, 71.

30. See the preface to my study, *Derech Gever, Siporet Homo Erotit Basifrut ha'ivrit hachadasha, 1880–2000* (Through Men: Homoeroticism in Modern Hebrew Literature, 1880–2000) (Tel-Aviv: Sufhra Publishing, 2003).

31. Ran Reznick and Ayelet Shahar, "From the London Garden to Independence Park" (*Miginat London legan ha'atzma'ut*), April 23, 1993. The locations mentioned in the title are cruising areas for gays.

32. The *Back Cover* on July 1, 1994, commented on *Ha'ir*'s frequent coverage of gay issues—so much so, it said, "that readers may get the impression that heterosexuality is an old-fashioned perversion."

33. See July 2, 16, and 23, 1993.

34. "OK, So You Took a White Rooster" (*Tov, lakachta tarnegol lavan*), October 29, 1995, 58.

35. *Ha'ir* did not only criticize what it considered the offensive and non-democratic mixing of religion, politics, and civics. On a more positive note, it also explored alternative Judaic and other spiritual traditions. See three articles in the May 6, 1994, issue: Zohara Ron, "Idol Worship" (*Avodat elilim*), 48–51, Micky Meltz, "Uri-Gellerism Denouncers" (*Sholelei ha'uri gellerism*), 52–53; and Elly Yishay, "A Little Guro and a Little Carlebach" (*Ktzat guru, ktzat Carlebach*), 54–56.

36. Shiri Harpaz, June 8, 1989, 18–20.

37. For an eloquent literary expression of these sensibilities see Yosef Luidor's short story "Yo'ash," in *Sipurim* (Massada Publishing, 1976). The story was written during the 1910s.

38. A subsequent article about the alternative masculinity of pop idol Aviv Gefen is another manifestation of the same sensibility. The young singer, who is described as soft, feminine, and pacifistic, captured the imagination of Israel's youth. See Rona Shafrir, "The Media's Critique" (*Bikoret hatikshoret*), March 18, 1994, 118.

39. Gideon Sammet, *Ha'aretz*, August 8, 1994.

40. Taub, *Hamered Hashafuf*, 37.

41. April 27, 1990, 5.

42. According to a 1992 independent poll, *Ha'ir* was the most widely read local weekly in Israel, with 12.4 percent of national readership. See the cover of the June 12, 1992, issue.

43. For more on this, see the first chapter in Almog's book, "Hachazit hatikshortit" (The Media Front), 43–343.

44. Although these issues were handled critically before by various authors (S. Yizhar, Amos Oz, A. B. Yehoshua, Hanoch Levin), until the media revolution of the 1980s and 1990s, they remained confined to high-brow works whose more subversive lessons were not as widely disseminated or internalized by the culture at large.

45. October 24, 1986, 12–13.

46. On the important place of bereavement in Israeli culture, see Hannah Naveh, *Bi-shevi ha-evel: ha'evel bire'i hasifrut ha'ivrit hachadashah* (Tel-Aviv: Hakibbutz Hameuchad, 1993), as well as the discussion of it in Chapter 4.

47. Amit Dubkin, February 2, 1992, 35. The reference is to the mass suicide in 72 C.E. of Jewish zealots who rebelled against the Romans and holed themselves up in the Judean desert fortress of Masada. When the Romans closed in on them, their leaders convinced everyone to commit suicide rather than fall into the hands of the enemy. In the 1920s the story began to circulate among Jewish pioneering youth and was eventually adopted by many as an inspiring story of national resistance and honor.

Three years later, another Israeli scholar, Yael Zerubavel, published a critical book about Israeli national myths, *Recovered Roots: Collective Memory and the Making of Israeli National Tradition* (Chicago: University of Chicago Press, 1995).

48. "Haselebrities shel hashchol," Zohara Ron, January 1, 1995, 46.

49. "Tell Me" (*Sapri lee*), February 4, 2000. See also an earlier article about this by Sha'ul Adar, titled "The Pornography of Bereavement" (*Hapornografia shel hashchol*), about the media's morbid fascination with soldiers' funerals, April 29, 1994, 44.

50. A reference to the head of Likud, Binyamin "Bibi" Netanyahu.

51. The word is bastardized to reflect the distinct Arabic pronunciation that is often derided by Israelis who wish to make fun of Arabs.

52. The Allenby Bridge connects Israel and Jordan near Jericho and is the only exit from Israel available to Palestinians. The card means transfer in effect.

53. This is a reference to a real episode in the first year of the Intifada, during which Palestinians were buried alive by an Israeli bulldozer used by the army to clear away ruins of buildings that were blown up.

54. The illustration on the card shows a club being broken on the head of an Arab. The IDF property is the club. The "damaging" agent is the Arab's head.

55. Ran Reznick, "Gaza Is Not for Us" (*Lo rotzim aza*), June 12, 1992, 32–33.

56. Ya'ir Nehora'i, "Why We Lost in the Intifada" (*Lama hifsadnu ba'intifadah*), October 15, 1993, 46.

57. Moshe Ashlag, "The Diameter of the Stain" (koter haketem), December 18, 1992, 50–51. In addition to the military reference to a bullet, the title may also refer to a well-known poem by David Avidan, "The Stain Remains on the Wall" (*Haketem nish'ar al hakir*), which deals with moral responsibility.

58. "Great, Come Back Tomorrow" (*Yoffi, nehedar, tavo machar*), September 24, 1993.

59. "Misgad tov ze misgad met," Gadi Bloom and Haled Sa'ad, May 7, 1993, 37. The article title is a pun on the well-known Israeli racist saying—a good Arab is a dead Arab.

60. "Sadistim besherut hamdina," Gadi Bloom, June 11, 1993.

61. Eitan Nahmi'as-Glass, "The Planted Hand" (*Vehayad od netu'a*), February 5, 1993, 38–40.

62. "MERETZ Ideology" (*Idi'ologyat meretz*), December 4, 1992, 77.

63. After uniting with two other small parties, MAPAM and Shinuy in 1992, the newly created MERETZ won 12 seats in that year's elections, the most the party ever held. Its size enabled it to have a greater influence on politics. For more details, see the Parties Lexicon at http://www.politicsnow.co.il/lexicon/meretz.html.

64. *Ha'im anachnu demokratia ma'aravit?* March 25, 1994.

65. *Hadat shamra al ha'am hayhudi?* April 1, 1994.

66. *Tov lamut be'ad artzenu?* Gadi Elgazi, April 13, 1994.

67. "Had Gadia," *Tarbut Ma'ariv*, April 25, 1997, 14–15.

CHAPTER 3

1. Gil Hovav, "Stories from the Depths of Your Soul" (*Sipurim mehabetzim shel haneshama*), *Kol Ha'ir*, February 28, 1992. Eventually the stories were published in more respected media, such as the socialist daily *Davar*, the Tel-Aviv weekly *Ha'ir*, and the Jerusalem weekly *Kol ha'ir*.

2. Ibid.

3. Batya Gur, *Ha'aretz*, June 17, 1994 (no title).

4. Fabiana Hefetz, "Young Only Biologically" (*Rak hagil tsa'ir*), *Yediot Aharonot*, March 6, 1992.

5. Yehudit Orian, "A Smiley Pessimism" (*Letsanut merira upesimism mechuyach*), *Yediot Aharonot*, May 6, 1994.

6. See Laurence Silberstein, *The Postzionism Debates: Knowledge and Power in Israeli Culture* (New York: Routledge, 1999).

7. Abraham Balaban, for instance, predicated an entire study of contemporary Hebrew literature on some of its definitions and analyzed the works of Keret and others according to them. See *Gal aher basiporet ha'ivrit: siporet ivrit postmodernistit* (Keter: Jerusalem), 1995.

8. In 1996 David Gurevitch conclusively presented Keret as a postmodernist in his article "Recycled Dreams" (*Halomot memuhzarim*), in which he includes other writers, most notably Orly Castel-Bloom and Gafi Amir. See *Iton 77*, vol. 194, March 1996, 38–43.

9. Yehudit Orian, "A Smiley Pessimism," Fabiana Hefetz, "Young Only Biologically," Alon Gayer, *Ha'aretz*, June 12, 1994.

10. Batya Gur, *Ha'aretz*, June 17 (no title).

11. Gideon Sammet, *Ha'aretz*, August 19, 1994 (for the exact quote, see Chapter 4, note 5); Einat Avrahami, "Many Trailers—No Movie" (*Harbe bekarovim vehaseret enenu*), *Ma'ariv*, May 6, 1994; Liza Chodnovsky, "Do Black Holes Exist?" (*Ha'im kayamim chorim shchorim?*), *Iton 77*, August–September 1988; Gavriel Moked, *Ma'ariv* (*yoman Tel-Aviv*), December 18, 1998.

12. Yigal Schwartz, "Twice Inverted" (*Hafuch al hafuch*), *Ha'aretz sfarim*, May 14, 1997, 6.

13. Asher Reich, "Etgar Keret Doesn't Care" (*Le'Etgar Keret lo ichpat*), *Ma'ariv*, June 22, 1994.

14. I am referring to the classical definition by Wayne Booth, *The Rhetoric of Fiction* (Chicago: University of Chicago Press, 1961).

15. For reasons beyond the publisher's control the cover of the second edition was replaced with an original illustration of black lines over a pink background depicting a tranquil Tel-Aviv streetscape in which various small details are surrealistically warped or missing. The effect is similar to what I describe above.

16. See Frederic Jameson on Warhol and on the affect-leveling tendencies of postmodernism in general in *Postmodernism, or The Cultural Logic of Late Capitalism* (Durham: Duke University Press, 1991), 7.

17. See Gurevitch's discussion of kitsch in his article "Recycled Dreams."

18. The awkwardness of such anglicized syntax is diminishing in modern Hebrew due to the growing exposure to English. But in the beginning of the 1990s it was very jarring, especially in literature.

19. Gil Hovav, *Yediot Aharonot*, Feb. 28, 1992.

20. Arik Glassner writes that "Keret's heroes are not entirely losers. They are goody-two-shoes in a macho world, that is, losers in one context but part of the hegemony in another." "Reading *Gulliver's Travels* in Icelandic" (*Likroh et mas'ot guliver be'islandit*), *Ha'aretz*, January 28, 2004.

21. I am assuming the word refers to the small fruit or berry of a weed that is used in local Arab cuisine in Israel. *Hubz* means bread in Arabic.

22. Eva Illouz, *Consuming the Romantic Utopia: Love and the Cultural Contradictions of Capitalism* (Berkeley: University of California Press, 1997), 91.

23. Hefetz, "Young Only Biologically," and Dina Stein, "Anatomy of Escape Routes" (*Anatomia shel shviley briha*), *Davar*, May 1, 1992.

24. Although the Holocaust was obviously not the reason for the establishment of the State of Israel, which began as an idea in the late nineteenth century, it serves as an extreme example in this story of the kinds of abuses Jews suffered throughout modern history that inspired Zionism as a solution.

25. I am referring here primarily to the outrage and ridicule instigated by the 1987 Landau Commission's sanction of "moderate physical pressure" to be applied to suspects in a ticking bomb situation in the name of what the commission defined as "state security."

26. Much of Orly Castel-Bloom's stories are predicated on this. See Chapter 1 and the Conclusion for more on this.

27. My discussion on postmodern characterization here is based on a paper delivered by Nurit Buchweitz at the NAPH conference in Stanford, California, in June 2005 titled *The Evacuation of Character in Postmodernist Prose: The Case of Keret and Castel-Blum*.

28. Buchweitz does not analyze this particular story. I extrapolate from her more general discussion.

29. "I read [the works of Keret's generation] and I feel jealous. When I did similar things in my days the critics tore me to shreds. Keret is being taught at the university and will receive the Israel prize yet. . . . Keret's ability and that of his peers to express themselves this way vindicates my own failure." Yoram Kaniuk, "Like a Happy Apathy" (*Kmo adishut smecha*), *Ha'aretz sfarim*, Dec. 16, 1998, 6.

30. Gavriel Moked, *Yoman Tel-Aviv—Ma'ariv*, Dec. 18, 1998.

31. Later on, Keret collaborated on several comic-strip projects, like *Streets of Rage* (*Simta'ot haza'am*; Tel-Aviv: Zmora-Bitan Publishing, 1997). Some of his works were turned into actual comics, or illustrated novels. *Hakaytana shel kneller* (*Kneller's Happy Campers*), for instance, was issued as an illustrated

novel called *Pizzeria Kamikaze* (Gainesville, Fla.: Alternative Comics; London: Diamond, 2005).

32. Jameson, *Postmodernism*, 8.

33. I am using the literary designation of "romance" here in the sense of a "novel."

34. From an interview with Gil Hovav, "In Bed with Irit Linur" (*Bamita im Irit Linur*), *Kol Ha'ir*, October 18, 1991.

35. Ibid. Linur first wrote ten pages of the novel, which she then optioned to Zmora-Bitan publishers. She completed the book only after she signed a contract. The book sold an unprecedented 50,000 copies. Linur uses the more vulgar "fucks" for what I translated here as "sex."

36. Zvia Ben-Shalom lauded the political deficiencies in "Normal" (*Normalim*), *Al Hamishmar*, August 20, 1993. Ariana Melamed welcomed the romance and love in "A Most Satisfying Junk" (*hajunk hachi mehane shel hanefesh*), *Kan Darom–Shavu'on Ashdod*, April 4, 1997.

37. Even though the Gregorian calendar is widely used in Israel, holidays are still observed according to the Jewish calendar, including the Jewish new year, Rosh Hashana. Sylvester is observed by relatively few people, mostly Westernized, secular, and affluent Israelis who are well-traveled.

38. The simple fact that this was the first native Israeli generation for whom Hebrew was the first and only language had profound influence on the language. It expanded and flexed it as only native speakers can. Itzhak La'or, who criticizes Keret here, is not too impressed with *Palmach* Hebrew, which he regards as cheaply contrived. See Itzhak La'or, "Don't Know How to Stutter" (*Lo yod'im legamgem*), *Ha'aretz–Yomon Tel-Aviv*, November 13, 1998.

39. Gideon Sammet, *Ha'aretz*, August 19, 1994. Sammet distinguishes Keret, Castel-Bloom, and Linur as exceptions.

40. Einat Avrahami, "Many Trailers—No Movie."

41. See Chapter 1.

42. La'or, "Don't Know How to Stutter."

CHAPTER 4

1. *Ma haya kore im hayinu shochachim et dov* (What Would Have Happened If We Forgot Dov), (Hasifriya hachadasha, Hakibbutz Hameuchad Publishing, Sifre Siman Kri'a, 1992). Four of the stories appeared earlier in the literary publication *Siman Kri'a*, vol. 22, July 1991.

2. Iri Rikin, "Local Anxieties" (*Metsukot mekomiyot*), *Ma'ariv*, January 21, 1993.

3. Avi Katz, "And Everything Was the Same, Only It Looked Different" (*Vehakol haya oto davar, rak sheze nir'ah acheret*), *Ha'aretz*, January 29, 1993.

4. See Dan Miron, "Between Surface and Deeper Pains" (*Ben pnei hashet-ach lik'evei omek*), *Ma'ariv*, April 5 and April 9, 1993.

5. Gideon Samet, *Ha'aretz*, August 19, 1994. Samet directs his criticism primarily at the writing in *mekomonim*, the local newspapers. He writes: "The whole episode was a generational misfire. Everyone stuttered and used all sorts of stylistic mannerisms in writing, dress, speech, and missed the opportunity to affect the era in a meaningful way. The country at large dealt with [political and security issues, while its young made] all kinds of faces, gazed at their na-vels, rated pubs in Tel-Aviv . . . and busily produced cultural icons."

6. Miron also contrasts Taub's heroes to the "typical Israelis of our domi-nant literature, verbose and over-conscious, who frequently worry about na-tional and cultural issues," "Between Surface and Deeper Pains."

7. *Ma haya kore im hayinu shochachim et dov*, 125.

8. Miron makes this point too, "Between Surface and Deeper Pains." He does not mention romance at all, though.

9. Uzi Weil, *Bayom shebo yaru berosh hamemshala—Sipurei ahava* (Tel-Aviv: Am Oved/Yediot Aharonot/Sifre Hemed, 1991).

10. Amir Zuckerman, "Something Good Will Happen to You Soon" (*Bek-arov yikreh lecha mashehu tov*), *Ha'aretz—Tarbut ve Sifrut*, June 28, 1991.

11. Ricky Rivlin, "Love Not War" (*Ahava lo milchama*), *Moznayim*, May–June, 1991, p. 85.

12. "מעידות אל המתיקות," Yigal Sarna, "Soaring and Precise" (*Medayek umamri*), *Yediot Aharonot*, May 3, 1991.

13. Ely Yishay, "Refreshing" (*Mera'anen kaze*), *Kol Ha'ir: Yerushalayim*, April 12, 1991.

14. A collection of excerpts from *Ha'ir's Back Cover* was recently published in Israel. See *The Life and Death of the Back Cover* (*Chayav umoto shel hasha'ar ha'achori*), Yediot Sfarim, 2006.

15. The Hebrew title of the dialogue is "Gvulot hata'am hatov." It appeared on March 3, 1996.

16. A well-known documentary about the Holocaust bearing the title "Be-cause of That War" was released a few years earlier in 1988.

17. "Uzi the journalist is almost an opposite mirror image of Weil the writer . . . for years he has been writing the satirical pages of *Ha'ir* with tre-mendous talent [while at the same time he has proved to be] a sensitive writer whose works are very melancholy." Nir Amprimi, *Iton Yerushalayim—Shavu'on Yerushalayim*, May 16, 1997.

18. *Ad gil 21 tagi'a layareyach*, Jerusalem: Keter Publishing, 1997.

19. Alona Kimchi, *Yediot Aharonot—Shiv'a Yamim*, November 22, 1996, 31–38.

20. Amir wrote for the youth magazine *Ma'ariv Lano'ar*, for the youth sup-plement of *Yediot Aharonot*, *Rosh beRosh*, and for the IDF youth publication,

Bamahane Gadna. Her first novel was *Ad klot* (*To the Very Ending*, Zmora-Bitan, 1987). See an interview with Nir Bachar, "Hip-hop, Tra-la-la," in *Kol Ha'ir*, May 22, 1995.

21. The usual translation of *stam* as "just because" is changed here to these new meanings. In addition to the works listed above, Amir wrote two more novels before publishing her fourth work which I discuss here: *Lotzchim* (*Don't Need to*, Tel-Aviv: Alfa/Zmora-Bitan, 1988), and *Tavasim al hagag* (*Peacocks on the Roof*, Tel-Aviv: Alfa/Zmora-Bitan, 1992).

22. *Ha'olam Haze* ran between 1937 and 1990 under several names. In the first few decades after 1948 it included an acerbic gossip column, "Rachel Gossips about Everyone" (Rachel merachelet al kol ha'olam) with behind-the-scenes tidbits about the country's leading politicians and socialites. See Asafa Peled, "Yellow Fever" (*Kadachat tsehuba, 7 Yamim* [weekend supplement of], *Yediot Aharonot*, February 6, 1998, 65–74).

23. Nir Bachar, "Hip-Hop, Tra-La-La."

24. Ibid.

25. Alona Kimchi, Yedi'ot Aharonot/Shiva Yamim, 31–38.

26. Nir Bachar, "Hip-Hop, Tra-La-La."

27. The word used for choices, אפשרויות, also means opportunities in Hebrew.

28. Eva Illouz, *Consuming the Romantic Utopia*, p. 95.

29. Ibid., 154.

30. American teenage soap opera that was very popular in the first half of the 1990s.

31. Amir transliterates the English in Hebrew letters, underscoring Ilanit's simplicity.

32. Crystal was a character on a long-running American soap opera, *Dynasty*.

33. Illouz, *Consuming the Romantic Utopia*, 30.

34. Ariana Melamed, "Read and Weep" (*Likroh kedei livkot*), *Ha'ir*, December 13, 1996.

35. Ibid.

CONCLUSION

1. Keret published another anthology of short stories, *Paper Moon*, in 2002. His 2004 *Pizzeria Kamikaze* is a graphic novel version of his 1998 *Kneller's Happy Campers*. Taub only published one belletristic book. After 2000 he published several children's books, like Uzi Weil. Gafi Amir's last novel is the 2001 *Dash Mine'uraich* (Farewell from Your Youth).

2. Orly Castel-Bloom was asked about this very phenomenon during a retrospective interview in the summer of 2007: "In the last few years the short story

has somewhat disappeared from Israeli literature and young writers [as opposed to you and your contemporaries] publish novels right away." Her reply is not conclusive. See Vered Lee, "Ani bati lahem behafucha," *Ha'aretz Sfarim*, August 15, 2007.

3. Tel-Aviv: Am Oved, 2000.

4. Tel-Aviv: Zmora-Bitan, 2002.

5. Or-Yehuda: Zmora-Bitan, 2004.

6. Or-Yehuda: Zmora-Bitan, 2005.

7. Tel-Aviv: Kinneret.

8. *Human Parts* (Boston: David R. Godine Publisher, 2003).

9. Her 2006 *Textile* (Tel-Aviv: Hakibbutz Hameuchad, Sifre Siman Kri'a), continues in this more realistic vein as well.

10. See Chapter 1.

11. A similar device is used by Ya'acov Shabtai, for instance, in *Past Continuous*, in which the disintegrating Ashkenazi elite is held together only by the long and thin run-on sentences that go on for pages on end.

12. Time in the novel is conspicuously measured according to the Jewish calendar, not the Gregorian; the latter is more commonly used in Israel.

13. Castel-Bloom clearly admitted to it herself: "Until 1995 I was convinced that the building of the State is behind us. Only in 2001 did I understand for the first time that this was not so. The precarious security situations [of the second Intifada, Y. P.] made me feel historically responsible to write about the present in particular." See Vered Lee, "Ani bati lahem behfucha."

14. See for example the politics and poetry of one of its most expressive proponents, Sami Shalom Chetrit, in his representative collection of poems, *Shirim Be'ashdodit* (Tel-Aviv: Andalus, 2003).

15. Ka-tzetnik was the pen name of Yehi'el Dinur, a Holocaust survivor and author of several novels on the Holocaust that were very popular during the 1950s, 1960s, and 1970s. He used these words to describe Auschwitz in his testimony during the Eichmann trial in Jerusalem in 1961.

16. The background of Amir and No'a is never related. I am surmising it from their names and by the fact that their neighbor is identified as Mizrahi.

17. The same reasons may have motivated soldiers before the Lebanon war, but they were never presented as such in the culture's literature. This is precisely my point. See also the discussion in the Introduction about a similar dynamic that occurs on post-army trips of Israeli youngsters to the Far East.

18. In an interview, Leshem mentions a caricature that was published in the daily *Yediot Aharonot* on the eve of the withdrawal in which IDF soldiers in Lebanon were drawn as watchdogs. See Ariel Schnuebel, "Oleh Lilvanon" (Going to Lebanon), September 3, 2006, *Makor Rishon Ba'internet, Iton Yisre'eli Le'umi* at: http://www.makorrishon.net/show.asp?id=8202.

19. Avirama Golan, "It's Going to Be All Right: How the Israeli Left Gave Up on the Society and Forfeited the Peace" (*Veyihye tov*), *Ha'aretz*, August 8, 2006.

20. "On July 13, one day after the war broke out, Gaidamak realized that there are masses of people who will not be able to leave the north. By the night of July 17 he had already erected a well-stocked tent city with room for 3,200 people. In four days he doubled the number of available spaces. It took the State a little more time. A first meeting about it was held at the Prime Minister's office on August 2. After a while the government put up its own tent city on the outskirts of Tel-Aviv. It was in place on August 14, in time for the ceasefire." Amos Harel, "Chalutz Has Plans" (*Lechalutz yesh tochniyot*), *Ha'aretz*, July 10, 2006.

21. Doron Rozenblum, *Ha'aretz*, August 18, 2006.

22. A competing interpretation of the defeat in the second war in Lebanon is that it will eventually erase the civic and democratic values promoted by *Ha'ir* and will resurrect in force its nationalistic tendencies. Only time will tell.

23. Gideon Sammet, *Ha'aretz*, August 19, 1994. See Chapter 4, note 5, for the full quote.

24. "The Prime Minister, the secretary of defense and the chief of staff look for the appearance of solutions rather than solving the real problems. These tricks are not helping because the crisis is too real . . . and at any rate the distress and neglect that the war exposed." "Olmert Doles Out Money" (*Olmert mechalek kesef*), *Ha'aretz*, August 27, 2006.

BIBLIOGRAPHY

Al-Dror, Yosef. *Hamuvan me'elav.* Tel-Aviv: Yediot Aharonot–Sifre Hemed, 1998.

Almog, Oz. *Predah mi-srulik: Shinui arachim ba-elitah ha-yisre'elit.* Haifa University Press, Zmora-Bitan Publishing, 2004.

Amir, Gafi. *Lotzchim.* Tel-Aviv: Alfa/Zmora-Bitan, 1988.

———. *Tavasim al hagag.* Tel-Aviv: Alfa/Zmora-Bitan, 1992.

———. *Ad gil 21 tagi'a layareyach.* Jerusalem: Keter Publishing, 1997.

Arbel, Rachel, ed. *Kachol lavan bitzva'im.* Diaspora Museum/Am-Oved, 1996.

Avigur-Rotem, Gavriela. *Chamsin vetziporim meshuga'ot.* Tel-Aviv: Keshet, 2001.

Avni, Yossi. *Gan ha'etzim hametim.* Tel-Aviv: Zmora-Bitan, 1995.

Balaban, Abraham. *Gal aher basiporet ha'ivrit: siporet ivrit postmodernistit.* Jerusalem: Keter, 1995.

Brandes, Yochi. *Hagar.* Tel-Aviv: Yediot Aharonot, Sifre Hemed, 1998.

Busi, Dudu. *Hayareyach yarok bavadi.* Tel-Aviv: Am Oved, 2000.

Castel-Bloom, Orly. *Lo rachok mimerkaz ha'ir.* Tel-Aviv: Am Oved, 1987.

———. *Doli siti.* Tel-Aviv: Zmora-Bitan, 1992.

———. *Chalakim enoshiym.* Tel-Aviv: Kinneret, 2002.

———. *Textil.* Tel-Aviv: Hakibbutz Hameuchad, Sifre Siman Kri'a, 2006.

Chetrit, Sami Shalom. *Shirim Be'ashdodit.* Tel-Aviv: Andalus, 2003.

Di-Nur, Daniela, ed. *Tzalmania, Rudi Weissenstein—retrospektiva.* Am Oved, 2002.

Ehrlich, David. *Habkarim shel shlishi vechamishi.* Tel-Aviv: Yediot Aharonot, Sifre Hemed, 1999.

Flapan, Simha. *The Birth of Israel: Myths and Realities.* New York: Pantheon Books, 1987.

Gay, Peter. *Education of the Senses, The Bourgeois Experience: Victoria to Freud,* Volume I. New York: W. W. Norton & Company, 1984.

Grossman, David. *Ayen erech: Ahava.* Tel-Aviv: Hakibbutz Hameuchad, 1986.

———. *Sefer hadikduk hapnimi.* Tel-Aviv: Hakibbutz Hameuchad, 1991.

Gutfreund, Amir. *Sho'a shelanu.* Tel-Aviv: Zmora-Bitan, 2002.

Gutman, Nahum. *Ir ktana ve'anashim ba me'at*. Tel-Aviv: Dvir, 1999.

Hoffman, Yoel. *Halev hu katmandu*. Jerusalem: Keter, 2000.

Holtzman, Avner. *Mapat Drachim*. Tel-Aviv: Hakibbutz Hameuchad, 2005.

Illouz, Eva. *Consuming the Romantic Utopia: Love and the Cultural Contradictions of Capitalism*. Berkeley: University of California Press, 1997.

Jameson, Frederic. *Postmodernism, or The Cultural Logic of Late Capitalism*. Durham: Duke University Press, 1991.

Katzir, Yehudit. *Lematis yesh et hashemesh babeten*. Tel-Aviv: Hakibbutz Hameuchad, 1995.

Kenaz, Yehoshua. *Baderech el hachatulim*. Te-Aviv: Am Oved, 1991.

Keret, Etgar. *Tsinorot*. Tel-Aviv: Am Oved, 1992.

———. *Ga'agu'ai lekissinger*. Tel-Aviv: Zmora-Bitan, 1994.

———. *Simta'ot haza'am*. Tel-Aviv: Zmora-Bitan, 1997.

———. *Hakaitana shel kneller*. Tel-Aviv: Zmora-Bitan/Keter, 1998.

———. *Anihu*. Lod: Zmora-Bitan, 2002.

———. *Pizzeria Kamikaze*. Gainesville, Fla.: Alternative Comics; London: Diamond, 2005.

Leshem, Ron. *Im yesh gan eden*. Or-Yehuda: Zmora-Bitan, 2005.

Levy, Itamar. *Agadat ha'agamim ha'atzuvim*. Jerusalem: Keter, 1989.

Luidor, Yosef. *Sipurim*. Massada Publishing, 1976.

Magen, Mira. *Kaftorim rechusim hetev*. Jerusalem: Keter, 1994.

———. *Al takeh bakir*. Tel-Aviv: Hakibbutz Hameuchad, 1997.

Matalon, Ronit. *Ze im hapanim elenu*. Tel-Aviv: Am Oved, 1995.

———. *Sara, sara*. Tel-Aviv: Am Oved, 2000.

Michael, Sami. *Victoria*. Tel-Aviv: Am Oved, 1993.

Mintz, Alan, ed. *The Boom in Israeli Literature*. Hanover, N.H.: University Press of New England, Brandeis University Press, 1997.

Mohar, Eli. *Mehana'aseh be'irenu*. Tel-Aviv: Am Oved, 1994.

Morris, Benny. *The Birth of the Palestinian Refugee Problem, 1947–1949*. Cambridge and New York: Cambridge University Press, 1987.

Naveh, Hannah. *Bi-shevi ha-evel: ha'evel bire'i hasifrut ha'ivrit hachadashah*. Tel-Aviv: Hakibbutz Hameuchad, 1993.

Nevo, Eshkol. *Arba'a batim vega'agu'a*. Or-Yehuda: Zmora-Bitan, 2004.

Nevo, Gidi. *Ad Kan*. Tel-Aviv: Hakibbutz Hameuchad, 1996.

Oz, Amos. *Michael sheli*. Tel-Aviv: Am Oved, 1968.

———. *Al tagidi, layla*. Jerusalem: Keter, 1994.

Peleg, Yaron. *Derech Gever, Siporet Homo Erotit Basifrut ha'ivrit hachadasha, 1880–2000*. Tel-Aviv: Sufhra Publishing, 2003.

Polhemus, Robert. *Erotic Faith*. Chicago and London: University of Chicago Press, 1990.

Sabato, Haim. *Emet me'eretz titzmach*. Tel-Aviv: Yediot Aharonot, Sifre Hemed, 1997.

Segev, Tom. *Hamilion hashvi'i*. Jerusalem: Keter/Domino, 1991.

———. *1949, hayisre'elim harishonim*. Jerusalem: Domino, 1994.

———. *1967*. Tel-Aviv: Hakibbutz Hameuchad, 2005.

Shaked, Gershon. *Hasiporet ha'ivrit 1880–1980*. Keter, Hakibbutz Hameuchad, 1980.

Shalev, Meir. *Roman rusi*. Tel-Aviv: Am Oved, 1988.

Shavit, Ya'acov, and Gideon Bieger. *Hahistoria shel Tel-Aviv*. Tel-Aviv: University of Tel-Aviv Press, 2001.

Shimoni, Yuval. *Cheder*. Tel-Aviv: Am Oved, 1999.

Shohat, Ella. *Israeli Cinema: East/West and the Politics of Representation*. Austin: University of Texas Press, 1989.

Silberstein, Laurence. *The Postzionism Debates: Knowledge and Power in Israeli Culture*. New York: Routledge, 1999.

Taub, Gadi. *Ma hayinu osim im hayinu shochachim et dov?* Tel Aviv: Hakibbutz Hameuchad, 1992.

———. *Hamered Hashafuf*. Tel-Aviv: Hakibbutz Hameuchad, 1997.

Weil, Uzi. *Bayom shebo yaru berosh hamemshala—Sipurei ahava*. Tel-Aviv: Am Oved/Yediot Aharonot/Sifre Hemed, 1991.

———. *Le'an holech hazikaron achare she'anachnu metim?* Tel-Aviv: Zmora-Bitan, 1996.

———. *Osher*. Tel-Aviv: Modan, 2001.

Yehoshua, A. B. *Hashiva mehodu*. Tel-Aviv: Hakibbutz Hameuchad, 1994.

———. *Masa el tom ha'elef*. Tel-Aviv: Hakibbutz Hameuchad, 1997.

Yizhar, S. *Giluy eliyahu*. Tel-Aviv: Zmora-Bitan, 1999.

Zerubavel, Yael. *Recovered Roots: Collective Memory and the Making of Israeli National Tradition*. Chicago: University of Chicago Press, 1995.

INDEX

Warhol, Andy, 67; *Campbell's Soup* (painting), 67

War of Independence, 129

Weil, Uzi, 92, 104–112, 120; "An Almost Sweet Life" (*Chayim kim'at metukim*, story), 105; "And You'll Be Dead" (*Ve'ata tihye met*, story), 111–112; "The Day They Shot the Prime Minister Down" (*Bayom shebo yaru berosh hamemshala*, story), 92, 104; "The Limits of Good Taste" (*Gvulot hata'am hatov*, story), 108–111; "Something Good Will Happen to You Soon" (*Bekarov yikre lecha mashehu tov*, story), 105–108

Yehoshua, A. B., 94, 122, 127; *The Lover* (*Hame'ahev*, novel), 127

Yizhar, S., 122

Zandberg, Esther, 57

Zhakont, Amnon, 45